OSPREY COMBAT AIRCRAFT • 15

B-24
LIBERATOR UNITS
OF THE EIGHTH AIR FORCE

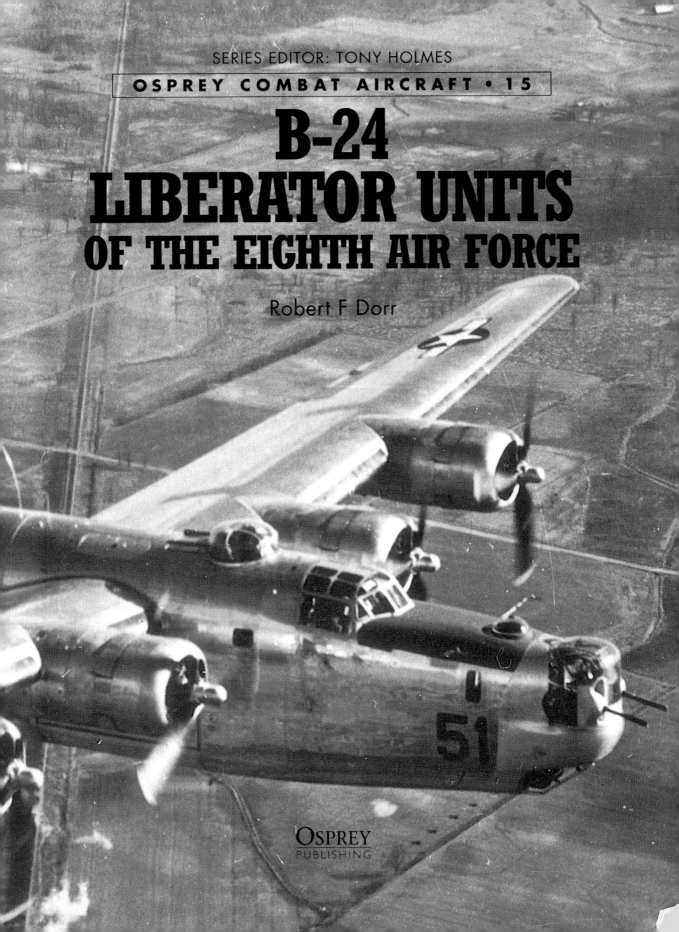

SERIES EDITOR: TONY HOLMES

OSPREY COMBAT AIRCRAFT • 15

B-24 LIBERATOR UNITS
OF THE EIGHTH AIR FORCE

Robert F Dorr

OSPREY
PUBLISHING

First published in Great Britain in 1999 by Osprey Publishing,
Midland House, West Way, Botley, Oxford OX2 0PH, UK
44-02 23rd St, Suite 219, Long Island City, NY 11101, USA
Email: info@ospreypublishing.com

Transferred to digital print on demand 2010

First published 1999
6th impression 2008

Printed and bound by Cadmus Communications, USA

A CIP catalogue record for this book is available from the British Library

ISBN: 978 1 85532 901 0

Edited by Tony Holmes
Page design by TT Designs, T & B Truscott
Cover Artwork by Iain Wyllie
Aircraft Profiles by Mark Rolfe
Scale Drawings by Mark Styling
Origination by PPS Grasmere Ltd., Leeds, UK

Dedication

This book is dedicated to the memory of T/Sgt Louis Marcarelli, who flew B-24 Liberator missions with the 791st BS/467th BG, Eighth Air Force, and who lost his life on 22 July 1944 after transferring to the Fifteenth Air Force

Acknowledgements

Any errors in this work are the responsibility of the author. Assistance in the preparation of this volume was received from the following B-24 crew members: Charles Deane Cavit (co-pilot 567th/389th BG), Alex Daniels (intelligence, 784th/466th BG), Ernest Davis (co-pilot 846th BS/489th BG), Lyman M Delameter (bombardier, 764th BS/461st BG), John Foster (radio operator, 846th BS/489th BG), Charles Frudenthal (bombardier, 489th BG), R F 'Dick' Gelvin (navigator, 700th BS/445th BG), Larry Herpel (pilot, 44th BG), Gene Hoffman (pilot, 329th BS/93rd BG), John A Jakab (pilot, 787th BS/466th BG), Will Lundy (inspector, 67th BS/44th BG), Charles A Melton (458th BG), Vince Re (gunner, 790th BS/467th BG), Edward K 'King' Schultz (pilot, 713th BS/448th BG); John E 'Jack' Stevens (pilot, 791st BS/467th BG), Horace S Turell (navigator, 703rd BS/445th BG) and Dale R Van Blair (gunner, 715th BS/448th BG).

Thanks also to Sigmund 'Alex' Alexander, Mike Bailey, Nathan Batoon, Allan G Blue, Warren M Bodie, Tom Brittan, Karen Cline, Carol Erbe, Wally Forman, Clyde Gerdes, Skip Guidry, William N Hess, Wade Hull, Tom Ivie, Kent Jaquith, Jim Kiernan, Sharon Kiernan, Dave Klaus, Wade Lovell, David R McLaren, A J Lutz, Sam McGowan, Ingemar Melin, Terrance D Olson, George A Reynolds, Jim Sullivan, Douglas E Slowiak, John Stanaway, Cindy Stevens, Norman Taylor, Ray Wagner, George Welsh, Michelle Welsh and Martin P Winter.

Front cover

Amongst the most famous early B-24Ds to see action with the Eighth Air Force during its first year in combat in the ETO were 41-23711 *JERK'S NATURAL* and 41-23722 *BOMERANG*, both of which served with the 328th BS/93rd BG 'Ted's Traveling Circus'. Depicted at the release point over a target in the spring of 1943, 41-23711 boasts an impressive mission tally board which features a variety of symbols, including a Shamrock leaf and a U-boat! The former denoted a visit to Northern Ireland to undergo modification work, whilst the latter signified a U-boat claimed as sunk by the crew of this aircraft whilst flying anti-submarine patrols over the Gulf of Mexico from Fort Myres, in Florida, in mid-1942.

Flown to Alconbury in September 1942 as part of the first wave of AAF B-24s to arrive in England, both *JERK'S NATURAL* and *BOMERANG* saw action from airfields in East Anglia and North Africa. The former was finally lost during a mission to Austria in October 1943, but 41-23722 lived on to complete 53 missions, prior to being sent back to the USA in April 1944 to undertake a War Bond drive tour.

Ironically, this aircraft had almost been written off following its very first mission in the ETO on 9 October 1942. One of 108 'heavies' (including 24 B-24Ds from 'Ted's Traveling Circus') sent to Lille to bomb the steel and engineering works of the *Compagnie de Fives* and the locomotive and freight car works of *Ateliers d'Hellemmes*, *BOMERANG* was shot up over the target. Its pilot, Lt John Stewart, nursed it back to Alconbury with approximately 200 holes in its fuselage and wings. The aircraft's groundcrew chief, M/Sgt Charles A Chambers, was literally beside himself with grief when he saw the condition of his formerly pristine bomber, shouting at its pilot, 'Goddamit, Lieutenant – what the hell you been doin' to my ship!' With few B-24 spares then available in the UK, it looked as if *BOMERANG* would end up being cannibalised for parts needed by other less seriously damaged Liberators. However, both Chambers and Stewart argued so vehemently against such a move that it was repaired and returned to flying status (*cover artwork by Iain Wyllie*).

FOR A CATALOGUE OF ALL BOOKS PUBLISHED BY
OSPREY MILITARY AND AVIATION PLEASE CONTACT:

Osprey Direct, c/o Random House Distribution Center,
400 Hahn Road, Westminster, MD 21157
Email: uscustomerservice@ospreypublishing.com

Osprey Direct, The Book Service Ltd, Distribution Centre,
Colchester Road, Frating Green, Colchester, Essex, CO7 7DW
Email: customerservice@ospreypublishing.com

www.ospreypublishing.com

CONTENTS

1942

When it was all over, and there was no going back to change any part of what had happened, Americans who fought over the continent in the Liberator wondered how in God's name they had endured the sub-zero cold, flak, fighters and the fickle cruelties of modern industrial warfare which gave the average crewman, according to one official estimate, only a 70-30 chance of coming out alive.

Many gave their lives. Others were wounded or held captive. It was a horror chamber – their situation, because of its constancy and repetition, in many ways more gruelling than the lot of any ground infantryman.

Then, there was the indignity. To add insult to injury, Liberator crew members lived forever in the shadow of what they mockingly called 'TOB', or 'that other bomber'. Studies show that the B-17 Flying Fortress is one of the 'most recognised' names in aviation where the general public is concerned, right up there with the Boeing B747 and the Supermarine Spitfire. In contrast, the B-24 – despite its numbers, its performance and its contribution – remains forever unknown to all except the *cognoscenti*.

Never mind that it was assembled in five factories (Consolidated at San Diego, California, and Fort Worth, Texas; Ford in Willow Run, Michigan; Douglas in Tulsa, Oklahoma; and North American in Dallas, Texas). Never mind that it was manufactured in greater numbers than any other US warplane of any era, the sum being 19,256 of all variants. The Consolidated B-24 Liberator (by other names the LB-30, F-7, C-87, C-109 and PB4Y-1) never got the press it warranted, nor did the veterans who maintained and flew it.

This great bomber owed its strength and success to a unique wing sold to Consolidated in 1937 by a near-destitute inventor by the name of David R Davis. Although the president of Consolidated, Reuben H Fleet, was sceptical, wind tunnel tests showed that Davis' slender wing with sharp camber provided superior 'lift'.

The prototype XB-24, which the manufacturer dubbed the Model 32,

The Consolidated B-24 Liberator never won the acclaim crews felt it deserved. It was always in the shadow of the prettier, but 'shorter-legged', Boeing B-17 Flying Fortress, even after it had become the most numerous military aircraft ever manufactured in the United States. In Europe, the strength and durability of the Liberator, and its ability to carry a huge bombload and to shoot back, were all pluses in the campaign waged by the Eighth Air Force. This rare aerial portrait depicts the first XB-24 prototype (39-556, later serialled 39-680) on an early test flight out of Consolidated's plant in San Diego, California (*San Diego Aerospace Museum*)

Long before Pearl Harbor, the United States was working hard to design, build and test four-engined bombers with ocean-spanning 'legs'. The Boeing XB-15 (35-227), seen here, and the Douglas XB-19, were two that proved exceedingly valuable as test ships, but never saw combat. This pre-war giant eventually ended up in Panama, redesignated as the XC-105 cargo aircraft. Boeing's leaner, slender B-17 Flying Fortress stole the show from the higher-flying, farther-reaching B-24 Liberator, leaving crews of the latter aircraft to feel that they were forever in the shadow of what they often called, simply, the 'other bomber' (*via Norman Taylor*)

shined in natural metal when completed its first flight, from San Diego, on 28 December 1939. With war already underway in Europe, the LB-30 export Liberator came ahead of US versions, and contributed to their development. As for the XB-24, it was powered by Pratt & Whitney R-1830-33 engines rated at 1100 hp. In March 1939 the US Army ordered seven YB-24 service-test bombers with turbo-superchargers for high-altitude flight. Next came nine B-24Cs, none of which saw combat, and the B-24D which fought everywhere. The turret-equipped B-24H model, appeared on 30 June 1943, followed by the B-24J, L and M, which had full gun armament, including nose turret.

CONDITIONS IN EUROPE

Ten thousand American bombers fell in battle during World War 2. A large chunk of that total consisted of B-24s of the Eighth Air Force. In looking back to those days when the sky was pungent with exhaust, black with exploding shellfire, and swarming with Messerschmitt and Focke-Wulf fighters, some men wondered simply how they had done it. Those who survived were destined to share a bond never experienced by those untested in battle, but their memories differed.

First version of the Liberator to see combat with the Eighth Air Force was the B-24D, seen here in a generic photo of B-24D-5-CO 41-23788 during a 1942 flight over California. The olive-drab camouflage and pre-August 1943 national insignia were standard. Note also the tyre from the main landing gear, which is flush with the lower surface of the Davis wing but not fully retracted. As combat crews were to quickly learn, the absence of a powered gun turret in the nose of the D-model was a handicap. All B-24Ds used the Pratt & Whitney R-1830-43 engine, except the late blocks produced at San Diego, which were powered by the -65 variant (*via Dave Klaus*)

On a bombing mission, where the risk of freezing was often as great as the danger of being shot, blasted or burned, one man recalled how the frigid temperature left skin from his penis attached to the relief tube. Another described seeing a single Liberator with 11 crew on board (one more than usual) disappearing in an abrupt, high-octane fireball. In the first bombing mission to Berlin, the number of Germans killed on the ground by bombs approximated the number of Americans killed in four-engined bombers high overhead.

Lt Col Frank Tribulent was a navigator with the 392nd Bombardment Group (BG);

'The conditions must have been the worst you could imagine. You wondered if you would get off the ground in the English fog with all those bombs on board. You wondered if you might collide with a buddy after you did. You worried that you'd drop a glove, or have a sleeve torn away, and get frostbite. And when the fighters were swarming around you, the adrenaline churned like crazy.'

In contrast to the Pacific, where crews flew missions in shirt sleeves (some of the time), B-24 Liberator flyers in Europe had to be bundled up against the elements. Crew member Lyman Delameter, a bombardier with the 461st BG, recalls;

'The B-24 was not pressurised like the B-29 Superfortress, and the aircraft that we fly today. We had to wear oxygen masks above a certain altitude (10,000 ft). I remember talking to one "veteran" aircrew member who advised me to wrap a towel around my neck like a scarf to collect the moisture that would accumulate under my chin from the oxygen mask. Of course, when we got to a higher altitude this moisture would freeze into a little ball of ice, and that would have to be cleared away from time to time.

'The old B-24 was not exactly airtight. The nose turret had to rotate from side to side, and the wind used to leak through the area where the nose turret joined the aircraft.

'The standard temperature lapse rate is two degrees colder per 1000 ft. So if the temperature on the ground was 40°, the temperature at 20,000 ft (6096 m) would be 40° colder. To compute the bombing altitude we had to know the temperature at this height.

'We had two types of flying clothing – sheepskin-lined leather pants and jacket and fur-lined boots, and the electrically-heated suit and shoes. The electrical heating wires in the suit were hooked in series. If one wire

'The box the B-17 came in', was the insult levied by Flying Fortress crews on the squarer, 'clunkier' Liberator. Those who faced flak and fighters in the B-24 countered by calling Boeing's product 'the smaller, older, slower bomber'. Still, no tale of Eighth Air Force bombers can hold up without at least this token shot of Vega-built Boeing B-17G-65-VE 44-8485 of the 100th BG, the 'Bloody 100th', seen at Haguenau Field, France, in 1944. In the early days, Eighth Air Force officers were glad to get any bombers they could. In late 1944, Lt Gen James Doolittle sought, with only limited success, to transform the 'Mighty Eighth' into an all-B-17 outfit (*Norman Taylor*)

By way of introducing the B-24 Liberator as a combat aircraft, this late-war portrait shows Ford-built B-24J-1-FO 42-50757 of the 855th BS/491st BG heading toward the Third Reich. By this juncture in the war – the photo is dated 1944 – the Liberator is attired in natural metal. However, the armoured plate slapped against the side of the fuselage to protect the co-pilot seems to have come from an aircraft painted olive-drab. The national insignia with bar was adopted in August 1943, and metal finish became standard several months later (*Norman Taylor*)

broke in that suit it would not work at all. It got darned cold the rest of the trip. The wires usually broke on the inside of the elbow, sometimes causing a small fire that would have to be slapped at a few times to extinguish. I looked up one day to see the nose gunner's door come open. He was beating out a fire in the elbow of his suit. I don't know what would have happened if a wire had shorted out in the crotch area.

'From time to time we would be briefed on the experiences of bomber crews that had bailed out and were able to evade and get back home. We were told that the heated suits did not work very well on the ground. If the heated shoes did not fly off from the opening shock of the parachute, they only lasted a mile or so before wearing out. For this reason, most of the guys tied their GI shoes to the parachute harness.'

FLYING AND FIGHTING

A further note about conditions. Crews had to worry about more than flak, Focke-Wulfs and Messerschmitts. For example, the necessity for oxygen created vexing problems. Navigator Horace Turell recalls;

'In my crew's 30 missions we never had a mechanical abort. Well, actually, we had only one, and I caused it. Early on I got my oxygen hose doubled and passed out with anoxia on the climb out. Same thing happened to our bombardier, only this time it was over the target, so I just turned his oxygen onto free flow and he came around.

'Every mission that was not maximum effort they would assign some spare to fill in for aborts. I did notice there was a higher abort rate on deep penetration missions. It was never more than two or three, and these were usually well justified. It was the pilot's call. For example, when you got over the sea and the gunners test fired, the nose turret guns would not fire, and could not be fixed in the air. Go on? Abort? Number four is running a little rough, same choice. We never had a plane where all systems worked perfectly. Just not possible.'

Americans like Turell were

Maj Gen Carl A 'Tooey' Spaatz was home in Alexandria, Virginia, when the telephone rang with the news that Japan had attacked Pearl Harbor. 'Christ, no!' uttered Spaatz, learning that Americans were now in a war many wanted to ignore. Spaatz commanded the Eighth Air Force from 4 May 1942 through to 30 November 1942, although he relied heavily on Maj Gen Ira Eaker, then boss of VIII Bomber Command, for the 'nuts and bolts' of evolving bombardment strategy. Spaatz was lukewarm toward Eaker's opinion (as expressed in a memo to Spaatz), that 'a large force of day bombers can operate without fighter cover against material objectives anywhere in Germany without excessive losses' (*USAF*)

everyday men in a 'citizen army' that had had a draft since 1940. Perhaps no one, themselves included, ever understood how they mustered the stuff for the job they faced. Apart from the terrible cold, the noise and the constant shaking, it was simply gruesome up there at a typical bombing altitude of 25,500 ft (7772 m), unable to dodge shells or debris after crossing the IP (initial point), flying in formation with aircraft ahead and above exploding in the air, with oxygen masks and body parts tumbling past the window, the swift black clouds of flak ever closer, the persistent Luftwaffe fighters on a collision course from dead ahead.

There was an insanity to it. Sometimes a Liberator came back with its insides smeared with vomit and blood. One navigator had a wooden box in which he kept as souvenirs the tagged metal pins removed from the blunt noses of bombs before dropping them. After the missions, those who did not need to be scraped out of the Liberator or rushed to the burn unit were given grapefruit juice, hard candy and rations of whiskey.

Alcohol flowed at the officers' club. At one station, when a man got drunk he was hoisted from his chair, his shoe bottoms were painted black, and he was turned upside-down and raised to a height so that the shoe impressions would darken the white ceiling. When the Eighth Air Force's 'thousand-day war' finally ended, the ceiling was black.

Each man's choice of words about what it was like to fly and fight in the Liberator in Europe has a different lilt, a different tang, but the immediacy

The first Liberators in England were glass-nosed, olive-drab B-24D models which lacked the nose turret installed on later versions. This dramatic shot of bombers traversing mud en route to a mission from Shipdham depicts B-24Ds from the 44th BG, whose 'Flying Eightballs' insignia is readily visible on the nose of the lead aircraft. The latter is believed to be B-24D-5-CO 41-23818 *BELA* of the 67th BS/44th BG, which was lost on 16 February 1943 following its involvement in a mid-air collision with another Liberator off Selsey, on the Sussex coast (*Planet via Will Lundy*)

Cheerful, impertinent, and lethal, the 'Flying Eightball' symbol of the 44th BG was derived from the most important ball in the game of pool. Seen at the group's base at Shipdham, this likeness was painted on 68th BS B-24D-20-CO 41-24282, which crashed with the loss of its entire crew at Eastbourne, Sussex, on 2 February 1944. Colours appearing on the nose of the 'Flying Eightball' emblem were broken down by squadron as follows: red (66th BS), yellow (67th BS), white (68th BS) and green (506th BS). The emblem (what would be called a 'logo' in future years) was designed by Maj Henry V Hart (then 44th BG Intelligence Officer) during August or September 1942, while the air echelon was at Grenier Field, New Hampshire, just prior to leaving for England (*via Will Lundy*)

and the fear and the horror shine through. And they did it all as part of an outfit that was, superficially, simply another 'numbered air force' among many, although it grew to become the mightiest air armada of all time.

EIGHTH GENESIS

As Americans saw it (often forgetting that their British friends had been fighting for more than two years before they began), they were going to use the British Isles as a stepping stone for a war that would eventually lead to an invasion of occupied Europe and the defeat of Germany. Although poorly prepared for war, and slow in spinning up the capabilities of their enormous industrial heartland, America had 'big bombers' (no other nation had as many four-engined 'heavies') and big ideas. From the beginning, some of the Army Air Forces' top officers must have sensed that the Eighth Air Force would become as vast as their dreams.

One veteran described the Eighth Air Force's humble beginning this way;

'Men of vision could see putting a thousand bombers in the sky over Europe. But when Ira Eaker went to England, he had five guys with him, and that was what they started with.'

It was not Eaker, of course, but Maj Gen Carl 'Tooey' Spaatz who first commanded Eighth Air Force (from 5 May 1942), but Eaker, who headed up Bomber Command under Spaatz, before relieving him in the top job (on 1 December 1942), was the bomber boss in England virtually from the start.

Eaker, and the others, wore the uniform of the Army Air Forces (AAF), a branch of the United States Army. The war would be fought and won without Americans having an air force as a separate service branch. To

Crews new to the Liberator started out with olive-drab (OD), 'plain jane' B-24Ds like these, which they used for rehearsing formation flying and group bombing in the friendly flying climate of the American south and southwest, before subsequently ferrying the aircraft to England. This previously unpublished study was almost certainly taken 'stateside' (although it could depict an arrival in England), and shows the standard OD paint scheme, the post-Pearl Harbor but pre-June 1943 national insignia, and not much else. These aircraft were olive-drab except for the undersurfaces of the fuselage and wings, which were painted neutral grey
(*Bill Eggleston via Robert F Dorr*)

forever confuse historians, these men were simultaneously members of both the AAF and the Army Air Corps. The latter term applied to the people throughout the conflict, while the people, aeroplanes, guns, bombs and bases all belonged to the AAF. Contrary to millions of words published in history texts, the term was not 'USAAF', and was never preceded by a 'US' prefix. Army Air Forces was always plural.

With a handful of men creating what was to become history's greatest air armada, Eighth Air Force (correct style was to spell the word, not render it as 8th) evolved into an organisation with four principal components – Air Service Command, Ground-Air Support Command, Fighter Command and Bomber Command. The four were usually identified by a roman numeral eight (VIII) before their titles. Eaker's VIII Bomber Command would itself evolve, and would in due course have two B-17 Flying Fortress units for every B-24 Liberator outfit. And under this headquarters in a year's time there would be formed three air divisions, with the 2nd Air Division having responsibility for most B-24 combat wings, groups and squadrons – but that command structure lay in the future.

There were future luminaries among the men who accompanied Eaker to England. They included a junior officer, Capt Beirne Lay Jr, who would later command the 487th BG. Another key figure in this story was Col Frank Armstrong, commander of the 97th BG. He later became the only general to command a bomb group in the Eighth Air Force when he took over the 306th BG in January 1943. Armstrong was the main inspiration for Beirne Lay and Cy Bartlett's character Gen Frank Savage in their classic novel *12 O'Clock High*. When somebody had to lead the

'They looked so young, but they got old quick', said one crew member who spoke truthfully, if not grammatically. S/Sgt Harold S 'Dutch' Erbe (front row, extreme left) flew as an engineer gunner with these Liberator crewmen in the 579th BS/392nd BG. This crew portrait leaps ahead of our story somewhat – Erbe and his crewmates went into action in 1943, and continued into 1944 – but it illustrates the quiet determination and the rude setting of American B-24 Liberator flyers as the Eighth Air Force grew in size and began to make an impact on the European conflict (*Carol Erbe*)

B-24 Liberator crew members from the 44th BG suit up to go to war at high altitude. Note the 'Flying Eightball' patch on the jacket worn by the crewman to the right, and the 'EB' monographed headwear of his buddy. The Eighth Air Force grew into the mightiest air armada ever, but its achievements were always those of men, not aeroplanes. More than 100,000 of them fought the daylight, high-altitude, war over Adolf Hitler's 'Fortress Europe', and for many the dangers of flight, including the cold, were as much a foe as the flak or fighters of the Third Reich. Exposure suits, Mae West lifejackets, leather jackets (which would be priceless if they survived today) and other gear all made a Liberator crew member's attire bulky and cumbersome (*via Dave Klaus*)

Eighth's Air Force's first heavy bomber mission over Europe on 17 August 1942, Armstrong drew the job. That mission was flown by the B-17 Flying Fortress.

BOMBING PLAN

The Americans came to England prepared to use B-17s, and the B-24 Liberators that soon followed, to bomb German-occupied Europe by daylight. At first, they intended to do this with minimal or even no fighter escort. The Royal Air Force, whose Lancaster and Halifax crews had already garnered considerable experience pounding the continent during the nocturnal hours, scoffed at daylight bombing.

'Overpaid, oversexed, and over here', was the hackneyed, if good-natured, complaint about Americans swarming into the British Isles, but some also wondered if they were all crazy. A bombing campaign conducted in daylight was a daft enough scheme, many Britons suspected, to earn its supporters lodging in that one-time madhouse on the far side of London's River Thames called Bedlam.

But nothing other than daylight bombing was seriously contemplated at Eighth Air Force headquarters at Bushy Park (code name *Widewing*), where Spaatz set up shop. Here, Spaatz established the 1st Bomb Wing (B-17s) and soon afterward the 2nd Bomb Wing, which arrived from the US in September 1942, and began functioning at Old Catton as the

Lt Gen Ira C Eaker became commander of the Eighth Air Force on 1 December 1942, replacing Maj Gen Carl A 'Tooey' Spaatz. Eaker had earlier been commander of VIII Bomber Command. Sometimes charged with not appreciating the importance of fighter escorts, Eaker is one of only three officers to have been advanced to the four-star rank of general after retirement, along with James H Doolittle and Benjamin O Davis. Relations between Eaker and Doolittle were correct – well acquainted for decades, they addressed each other not by first name, but as 'General' (*AAF*)

An excellent study of nose details of the B-24D – the model of Liberator in which crews began air operations over Europe in late 1942. The nose arrangement in the D-model may have offered up too many machine guns, for the navigator and bombardier were at each other's elbows when simultaneously manning the three Browning 0.50-cal. (12.7-mm) weapons protruding forward and from both sides. This resulted in too narrow a field of fire for the trio of weapons. *Princess*, also known at various times in its career as *Princass* and *Prince*, was a Fort Worth-built B-24D-10-CF (42-63962) of the 506th BS/44th BG (*via Will Lundy*)

parent unit for B-24 Liberator groups.

The first of these was the 93rd BG, which was destined to be in combat from 9 October 1942 until 25 April 1945, and to participate in 396 missions. The group was dubbed 'Ted's Traveling Circus', after its commander, Col Edward J (Ted) Timberlake Jr. Like all of the pioneers in the Eighth, their aircraft did not initially wear distinctive unit markings, although later in the year they acquired British fin flashes during 'detached service' in North Africa. In August and September 1943, the group acquired as its marking the letter 'B', encircled in white, on the fin. After May 1944, its bombers would fly in natural metal, with tails painted deep yellow with a black vertical stripe.

The 93rd consisted of four squadrons. As with all B-24 outfits in Europe, later in the war they acquired two-letter identifier codes, painted on the side of the fuselage. The units, and their future codes, were: 328th BS (GO), 329th BS (RE), 330th BS (AG) and 409th BS (YM).

The group's first base was at Alconbury, in Huntingdonshire. The airfield was also known as Station 102. The first Liberator crews to fly in arrived in dark olive-drab and neutral grey B-24Ds (this model lacking the nose turret fitted on all subsequent variants of the Consolidated heavy bomber), although some also had green blotching along the edges of flight surfaces on the wings.

9 October 1942 saw the debut of the Liberator over the continent. The newly-arrived 93rd BG contributed 24 B-24Ds out of 108 bombers (all others being B-17s) in a five-group assault against the French city of Lille. Principal targets were the steel and engineering works of the *Compagnie de Fives* and the locomotive and freight car works of *Ateliers d'Hellemmes*.

Timberlake took off at 0747 to lead the Liberator force at the controls of his B-24D-5-CO 41-23754, nicknamed *TEGGIE ANN*. P-38 Lightnings and Spitfires went along. It was a milestone in the early growing pangs of the fledgling Eighth Air Force – namely the first time more than 100 heavy bombers were despatched on a raid. The Luftwaffe was ready with an aggressive mix of Messerschmitt Bf 109s and Focke-Wulf Fw 190s, which made more than 70 passes at the bombers in a running, 30-minute, duel.

Sgt Arthur Crandall, a gunner with the 93rd BG, shot down an Fw 190

near Lille that day. He was part of the crew for B-24DD-1-CO 41-23667 *BALL OF FIRE*, flown by Capt Joseph Tate. While over the target, three Focke-Wulfs attacked the bomber and fired a shell through its right vertical stabiliser. At about this time Crandall was credited with shooting down 'his' Fw 190, which appears to be the first victory credited to the Eighth Air Force – Crandall was later shot down on 16 April 1943 in *BALL OF FIRE JR.* over Brest, becoming a PoW.

Although Arthur Crandall's assigned duty was as a tail gunner, group records do not make it clear as to whether he was manning that position when he claimed the 93rd BG's historic first kill. This success was tempered by the fact that the group lost a B-24 during the mission.

One 93rd BG officer who participated in the first raid was 1Lt Ramsay Potts, who would later command the group's 330th BS, and rack up an impressive list of achievements as a Liberator pilot and leader. Soon afterward, Potts' first claim to fame was when his lone Liberator was attacked by five fighters over the Bay of Biscay while flying an anti-submarine mission. His crew shot down two Junkers Ju 88s, and Potts dived into the clouds, giving the others the shake.

One final note about terms: although Liberators acquired colourful portraits on their noses while en route to the war, or after arriving amid the fighting, the term 'nose art' did not exist during World War 2, flyers simply referring to them as pictures, cartoons, nudes or whatever word was appropriate. Likewise, the aircraft did not have 'nicknames', since this term refers to an additional name, or a substitute for the real thing.

Although not taken in the Eighth Air Force area of responsibility, this underside view is worthy of inclusion for its illustration of the rarely seen 'belly' of an early B-24D. More than half a century later, the attics and basements of B-24 crew members are awash with close-up pictures of 'nose art' (a term that did not exist during World War 2) and of crews posing beside aircraft. However, complete views of aircraft in flight – especially B-24Ds – are almost impossible to find (*USAF*)

There were several bombers nicknamed *SPIRIT OF '76* within the Eighth Air Force – a reference to 1776, when American rebels fought British colonists in a war for independence – and the example depicted here is B-24D-5-CO 41-23776. This bomber was so named because of its serial. Typical of early Liberators thrown into the fray in Europe, this 68th BS/44th BG machine was posted missing in action on 27 January 1943. Only one of its crew survived the mid-air explosion which destroyed the bomber (*via Will Lundy*)

DOWN 'DE HATCH and *GLORY BEE* (the latter aircraft featuring in two photos, showing it both before and after acquiring mission markers) were operated by the 44th BG (*via Will Lundy*)

When an appellation was painted on the nose of a B-24 to reflect the pilot's, or the crew's, wishes, it was a name, not a nickname. Bomb groups, however, had nicknames in addition to their official designations.

ENTER THE 44th

When formed, the 44th BG had been the first Liberator combat group in the AAF. It was the second (behind the 93rd BG) to fly in the Eighth Air Force, where it was assigned to the 2nd Bomb Wing, which would evolve into the 2nd Air Division.

The 44th BG 'Flying Eightballs' joined the fray on 7 November 1942. The group's first operation consisted merely of seven Liberators creating a diversion for an attack elsewhere by Flying Fortresses. The 44th was destined to participate in 343 missions and drop 18,980 bombs between that date and 25 April 1945 – of the B-24 groups, only the 93rd BG racked up a higher tally of missions and delivered more ordnance. Over the course of the war, this group would lose an extraordinary 192 Liberators and claim 330 Luftwaffe fighters destroyed in return.

The group arrived in England with olive-drab B-24Ds. They initially lacked distinctive markings, although most acquired British tail flashes

Gen Henry H 'Hap' Arnold, the commanding general of the AAF (Army Air Forces), had overcome numerous hurdles in the prewar years in order to build a strategic force of four-engined heavy bombers. After the bombers went to work for the Eighth Air Force, Arnold visited frequently from Washington, and sometimes became involved in field-level decisions. Although there is a conflicting record of his opinion, Arnold seemed to prefer the B-17 Flying Fortress over the B-24 Liberator, and was reluctant to see the newer Consolidated bomber used in large numbers in Europe (*Norman Taylor*)

PISTOL PACKIN' MAMA, like so many Liberators, went through several combinations of nicknames and nose art. This aircraft was B-24D-160-CO 42-72858 from the San Diego plant, and it served with the 'Flying Eightballs' of the 44th BG, but not for long – replete with both caricature and nose art, *PISTOL PACKIN' MAMA* diverted to neutral Sweden and was interned 'for the duration' until being scrapped postwar (*via Will Lundy*)

for 'detached service' in North Africa. In September 1943, the 44th acquired as its group identifier a white disk bearing a blue capital 'A' on the upper starboard wing and fin. The group's squadrons, and their eventual codes, were as follows: 66th BS (QK), 67th BS (NB), 68th BS (WQ) and the 506th BS (GJ).

Home for the 44th BG was Shipdham, which was the first heavy bomber base used by the Eighth Air Force in Norfolk. Like the 93rd BG, the group would also operate aircraft on detached duty in North Africa in 1942-43. During their first sorties over Europe in 1942, the 'Eightballs' of the 44th took a drubbing from the Luftwaffe.

It would become clear that common sense demanded segregation between Flying Fortress and Liberator groups, bomb wings and, ultimately, numbered air divisions. As the first B-24 group to arrive in the Eighth, the 93rd BG 'Circus' was originally assigned to the 1st Bomb Wing, where it flew alongside B-17 outfits. But the B-24 Liberator was a faster aircraft, and was therefore at a considerable disadvantage when forced to retard its speed in order to stay in formation with 'that other bomber'. On 5 December 1942, the 93rd BG was placed alongside the 44th BG on the wiring diagram (organisation chart) as part of the 2nd Bomb Wing.

Within ten days of joining the 44th BG, the 93rd lost one of its squadrons, when the 329th BS shifted to Bungay, in Suffolk, on 14 December, and was ordered to prepare for special night intruder missions. Dubbed 'moling' sorties by the crews that flew them, the unit's primary role was to penetrate Hitler's 'Fortress Europe' in bad weather in order to alert enemy air raid and defence units of the potential presence of bombers, and therefore interrupt industrial production. The experiment was to be short-lived, and its contribution towards reducing the Third Reich's war production was questionable at best.

GROWING WAR

In late 1942, the dream of an aerial armada darkening the skies over Hitler's Germany was still a fantasy in the minds of a few leaders, but more B-24s were coming to join the battle as it grew. The 44th BG had been the second Liberator group to arrive in England, a few weeks behind the 93rd. No others were to join the fray in calendar year 1942, but in any event the Eighth was to be distracted by events in the Middle East.

On 20 October 1942, Gen Dwight D Eisenhower issued a directive reflecting the immediate urgency of Operation *Torch* (the invasion of North Africa), and requiring the Eighth Air Force, as a matter of first priority, to protect the movement of men and supplies from the United Kingdom to North Africa. This was to be done by attacking German submarine pens on the west coast of France, with shipping docks in the same area as secondary targets for these missions, and with German aircraft factories and depots in France assuming a lesser priority.

However, Spaatz informed AAF boss Gen Henry H 'Hap' Arnold that operations against sub pens might prove too costly for the results obtained. Believing the pens impervious to normal high-altitude bombing, Spaatz planned to operate as low as 4000 ft (1220 m) and accept higher casualty rates. The first missions were flown by B-17s, which still enjoyed greater confidence on the part of Eighth Air Force leaders.

The Liberator was getting off to a slow start, with two squadrons from the 93rd BG briefly on loan to Royal Air Force Coastal Command for anti-submarine patrols in the Bay of Biscay. On 21 October 1942, 'Ted's Traveling Circus' launched 24 Liberators on an intended low-level raid against U-boat pens at Lorient, in France, but because of 100 per cent cloud cover, they were unable to bomb the target. A mission to Brest by 12 Liberators on 7 November 1944 also produced little result, although it marked the first combat by the 44th BG, which launched seven aircraft in a diversionary effort.

Two days later, a mixed attack by 33 B-17s and 12 B-24s on St Nazaire resulted in the loss of three Fortresses and a Liberator, severe damage to nearly every aircraft that participated, and a major reassessment of using

It was done with the same formality as handing out wings or laminating an identity card. Crew after crew posed for these portraits of men and machine. This quartet of previously unpublished crew portraits depict members of the 44th BG (*via Will Lundy*)

heavy bombers to attack submarine facilities. Henceforth, the 'heavies' would bomb not from low altitude as Spaatz had done initially, nor from medium altitude of around 17,500 ft (5334 m) as on the St Nazaire raid, but from their optimum height of 25,500 ft (7772 m). At Bushey Park, there was some discussion of giving priority to other targets, and leapfrogging the submarine pens entirely.

The King of England visited the 93rd BG on 13 November 1942, this being George VI's first visit to an American heavy bomber group. The next day, the 93rd despatched 13 B-24s to accompany 21 B-17s for a revisit to St Nazaire from greater height, while the 44th mounted half a dozen Liberators as a diversion. Missions to Cherbourg and Lorient followed. Whilst attacking the latter target on 18 November 1942, B-24D-5-CO 41-23745 *KATY BUG* of the 93rd BG lost two engines and 'piled up' near Alconbury, killing six of the ten men on board. This did not prevent another strike on Lorient on 22 November 1942 in which 68 B-17s were accompanied by seven B-24s from the 'Circus'.

On 13 December 1942, the 93rd BG was uprooted from England and sent off to North Africa. On this occasion, it was shifted to the Twelfth

Air Force, although a later sojourn to the same region would place it under the purview of the Ninth Air Force, thus adding its Liberators to the aerial bombardment of Axis supply ports. In North Africa, the men found primitive facilities, furious winds, rain and mud. At one point, it was impossible to taxy a Liberator because the mud created such an obstacle. The 93rd BG eventually flew 22 missions over 81 days before returning to England. But another trip to North Africa lay in the future for 'Ted's Traveling Circus'.

The 44th BG completed 1942 in England by striking Abbeville on 6 and 12 December. Eight days later, a dozen Liberators from the 'Eight-balls' were able to join 71 Fortresses on a raid to a Luftwaffe supply centre at Romilly-sur-Seine. At the time, members of the 44th BG did not know that they, too, would soon find themselves in North Africa. Ahead lay a place that no Flying Fortress was 'long-legged' enough to reach – Ploesti.

1943

At the beginning of 1943, one 93rd BG officer who was on the 'fast track' was George S Brown, a future air force chief of staff. Brown commanded the 93rd BG's 329th BS, and had been assigned to 'top secret' work in the autumn of 1942. When the rest of the 93rd BG went to North Africa for the winter of 1942-43, Brown's squadron remained in England. On 2 January 1943, four 329th BS Liberators, including one flown by Brown, took off from England to perform the first penetration of German airspace ever undertaken by AAF bombers. It was called 'moling'.

Using RAF-provided navigational equipment, the four modified Liberators were to drop bombs through heavy overcast on Bremen, Hanover, and Osnabruck. But as the flight neared northern Germany, the weather suddenly cleared. Having been briefed to not risk allowing their classified equipment to fall in the hands of the Germans, the mission was scrubbed. They turned out over the North Sea and dropped their bombs. Censors placed restrictions on the news that American bombers had gone into Germany. The equipment used by the 329th, and the techniques developed within the squadron, provided the foundation for the PFF, or 'Pathfinder', bombing method that became so crucial to US heavy bomber operations after the autumn of 1943.

Brown later became deputy group commander of the 93rd BG. After finishing his combat tour, he transferred to 2nd Air Division headquarters,

No sight from the war years quite matched the stark drama of a formation of four-engined heavy bombers heading into harm's way. What might be mistaken for breaks in the typical European cloud cover actually include, in this photo, bursts of flak stalking these Liberators. The year is 1944, and the target is the Pas de Calais, in France. No target was ever an assured 'milk run' (the flyers' term for an 'easy' mission), and this French objective clearly turned out to be anything but easy (*via Neal Schneider*)

POOP DECK PAPPY was Ford-built B-24H-1-FO Liberator 42-7521 of the 577th BS/392nd BG. It is seen here flying high over Norwich, in Norfolk, upon its return from an 10 October 1943 mission to Oslo, in Norway. The national insignia shown, with its insignia red surround, had already been out-of-date for more than a month when this photo was taken, having been replaced by a marking with a blue border. Note the wavy separation between the olive-drab upper surfaces and the light gray undersides. *POOP DECK PAPPY* later flew with both the 44th and 448th BGs, surviving its spell in the frontline to be RZI (Returned to the Zone of the Interior USA) with the latter group *(via Warren M Bodie)*

and from there back to the newly-constructed Pentagon building in Washington, DC.

On 12 March 1943, the 329th BS returned to control of the 93rd BG, its three-month experiment with 'moling' (penetrating enemy skies at night and in bad weather to 'tweak' German defences) regarded as something less than a success.

In the meantime, B-24s had continued sporadic attacks on St Nazaire. On 3 January 1943, the 44th BG had three Liberators crash-land with fuel shortages whilst returning home from bombing the submarine pens.

On 27 January, 20 bombers from the 44th BG, plus seven from the 93rd BG, joined 64 Fortresses in a strike on the Wilhelmshaven naval base. Plagued by poor weather and formation problems, only half of the bombers released their ordnance over the target. In fact, not one of the Liberators was effective due to a 'hodgepodge' of navigational and weather errors. Still, it was the first conventional bombing of German soil by American 'heavies'.

On 15 February, two-dozen Liberators from the 44th and 93rd BGs bombed Dunkirk. The next day, when Fortresses and Liberators returned to St Nazaire, two 'Eightball' B-24s collided over the English Channel.

After an 8 March mission to Rouen, which produced mediocre results, a more ambitious mission was mounted on 14 May 1943 when 136 bombers, including 21 Liberators, struck the Kiel shipyards. It was a bloody day for the 44th BG, which lost six B-24s, including one that went into the sea after the crew had bailed out. The 'Eightballs' were given their first Distinguished Unit Citation for paying a heavy price on this raid.

There were other raids to Bordeaux and La Pallice, but the campaign against U-boat facilities was about to be eclipsed by another priority.

ENTER THE 389th

Known as 'The Sky Scorpions', the 389th BG formed in England on 9 July 1943 under the command of Col Jack W Wood, and was immediately sent on 'detached service' to Libya.

The group was initially equipped with B-24Ds, and during the course of the war also flew H-, J-, L- and M-models. After detached service in North Africa, the 'Scorpions' resided at Hethel (Station 114), in Norfolk.

The 389th BG was made up of the 564th BS (later to acquire the letter code YO), 565th BS (EE), 566th BS (RR) and 567th BS (HP). A Liberator outfit throughout the war, and 389th BG went from olive-drab to natural-metal aircraft in much the same way many other bomb groups did. Ultimately, the 389th BG flew 321 missions, completing its final operational foray over Germany on 25 April 1945.

Shortly after Lt Col Addison 'Bake' Baker replaced the much-admired Ted Timberlake as boss at the 93rd BG (on 17 May 1943), a mysterious field order, dated 1 June 1943, from the 2nd Air Division put an abrupt halt to Liberator operations over Europe.

Crews were suddenly given new N-7 low-altitude bombsights and put to work practising low-level flying over the British countryside. Baker led a brace of Liberators on a treetop-level sweep using hangars at Hardwick as a mock target. New machine-gun installations were rigged on B-24Ds with hand-swivel mounts. Throughout the Eighth Air Force's Liberator bomb groups – 44th, 93rd and the soon-to-arrive 389th – everybody wondered what was going on.

Also in that category were English farmers. Cows became upset when Liberators skimmed over their heads, barely fence-high. The bovine herds probably knew about as much as Liberator gunners and radiomen, who were aware that a secret mission was brewing, and speculated that they were practising to attack the German battleship *Tirpitz*, hiding in a Norwegian fjord. Others were sure they were preparing to strike the Brest

The 1 August 1943 the B-24 force sent to strike at the huge oil refinery complex at Ploesti, in Romania, saw the combination of two bomb groups from the Ninth Air Force (98th, 376th BGs) and three from the Eighth Air Force (44th, 93rd and 389th BGs), the latter on 'detached service' from England. This painting by Bob Hill, used with his permission, shows B-24D-1-CO 41-23722 *BOMERANG* (also depicted on the cover) over the target, accompanied by B-24D-1-FO 41-23717 *Exterminator*, which did not make it back. Both belonged to the 328th BS/93rd BG. *BOMERANG* later became the first 'Mighty Eighth' Liberator to complete 50 missions (*Bob Hill*)

submarine pens. They could not have been more wrong.

The 1 August 1943 low-level mission against Axis oil refineries in Ploesti, Romania, (carried out by five bomb groups, including three on 'detached service' from the Eighth Air Force) is recounted in greater detail in the *Combat Aircraft* volume pertaining to Liberator units in service with the Ninth, Twelfth and Fifteenth Air Forces. Suffice to say that for a brief juncture there would be no Liberators in England, and no Liberator operations being mounted by Eighth Air Force against the continent. This did not mean life was easy: the treetop-level training was gruelling, and on 18 May two Liberators of the new 389th BG collided whilst flying in a three-aircraft element

When he arrived in England on 11 June 1943 to take over command of the 389th BG, Col Jack W Wood found that his first task was to increase the intensity of the low-level 'beating-up' of the English countryside.

The 93rd BG, now commanded by Lt Col Baker, left England in late June 1943, followed soon afterwards by the 44th and 389th BGs. At five rudimentary 'bases' around Benghazi, in Libya, they attempted to adjust to conditions that were very different from those in England. Although not directly hit, the groups were nearby one night when Italian saboteurs

These aeroplanes, and this base, are not Eighth Air Force, but this image of whirling propellers and swirling sand illustrates conditions that were encountered by the Eighth's 44th, 93rd and 389th BGs when they joined the *Tidal Wave* operation. This B-24D Liberator of the 376th BG, Ninth Air Force, is returning to Benghazi, Libya, following the 1 August 1943 attack on Ploesti. The Ninth Air Force participants wore sand-coloured camouflage, while the Eighth Air Force bombers on the raid retained their olive-drab finish (*USAF*)

Another illustration of the sand-coloured paint scheme on Ninth Air Force B-24D Liberators that struck Ploesti on 1 August 1943. This aircraft is B-24D-1-CO 41-23766 of the 98th BG, and is presented here as typical of the bombers that accompanied 'detached service' Eighth Air Force Liberators to the target (*Norman Taylor*)

landed from a midget submarine, killed two Americans and blew up four aircraft! More importantly, while they had always carped about the clouds and rain in England, now they cursed the winds and the sand.

On 'detached service', and no longer carried on the Eighth Air Force's books, the Liberator squadrons from England flew a few missions (ten by the 44th and 93rd BG, and six by the 389th) as part of Operation *Husky*,

One last look at Ploesti – and one final photo that is not of the Eighth Air Force, but symbolises a warplane, and a target, that live in history. The most famous photo ever taken of the B-24 Liberator was shot over the Concordia Vega oil refinery complex at Ploesti – but not on the 1 August 1943 mission and, indeed, not until much later in the war on 31 March 1944. By then, the 'second front' Fifteenth Air Force was a big-time operator of heavy bombers. The rest of the Liberator story in the Mediterranean with the Ninth, Twelfth and Fifteenth Air Forces will be the subject of a separate volume in this series (*AAF*)

B-24D-1-CO Liberator 41-23722 *BOMERANG* of the 328th BS/93rd BG. This famous bomber was delivered to the AAF on 23 July 1942, *BOMERANG* inadvertently having an 'o' omitted from the spelling of her nickname by a painter at Grenier Field, New Hampshire, who affixed the nose art while the bomber was headed overseas. The aircraft flew the 9 October 1942 mission to the Lille steel works in France, went on detached service to accomplish the 1 August 1943 strike on Ploesti, and then returned to England to become the first Eighth Air Force Liberator to complete 50 combat missions (*Kent Jaquith*)

With the Eighth Air Force growing in size and expanding its reach, the training of Liberator crews accelerated at bases around the United States. By early 1943, the AAF had begun steps to train B-24 pilots and crews at 12 bases across the country. Thus, flyers learned about their aircraft in weather that was far more congenial than the conditions awaiting them in Europe. This formation of B-24D Liberators in early 1943 is typical of the myriad training flights that took place (*Kent Jaquith*)

supporting the Allied landings in Sicily. On the first such mission on 2 July 1943 against airfields in Italy, 1Lt Robert Lehnhaisen's B-24D (of the 44th BG) sustained numerous hits and crashed into the sea. A British minesweeper sent a life raft that saved Lehnhaisen and several of his crew.

A total of 124 Liberators were sent out from England to the North African desert – not one was left behind in the Eighth Air Force's home 'jurisdiction'. But in their absence, civilian contractors across East Anglia were building more airfields, and expanding and improving existing ones.

The men 'detached' from England now flew and trained alongside two Liberator groups belonging to the Ninth Air Force (and soon to join the fledgling Fifteenth). These were the 376th BG 'Liberandos', under Col K K Compton, and the 98th BG 'Pyramiders', under Col John 'Killer' Kane. Two more spirited leaders, or two more different men, would have been difficult to find, Compton being viewed as more relaxed and easygoing, even though a stern taskmaster, whilst Kane was almost totally lacking in warmth, but without peer as a leader and flyer.

Together with the very experienced, and much-loved, Leon Johnson of the 44th, the very capable Baker of the 93rd and newcomer Wood of the 389th, these men – indeed, all of the men in the five B-24 heavy bombardment groups – prepared for one of the most extraordinary

operations staged during World War 2. And they started with further practice – more and more of the gruelling training flights over the Libyan sands. Even a blind man could have guessed that the B-24s were preparing for a secret mission, flying so low they scraped their bellies on the desert.

The Allies were convinced that sending a fleet of heavy bombers against German oil production would strike a major blow, and alter the course of the war. The previous year, on 12 June 1942, B-24s belonging to an outfit called Halpro had become the first American heavy bombers to attack 'Fortress Europe' with a mission against the oil refineries at Ploesti. With a much larger Liberator force now available to the Allies in North Africa, a much more ambitious raid against Ploesti was planned. It was all very secret, but it was not difficult to figure out. The second attack on Ploesti was to be code-named *Tidal Wave*.

Although the event took place on the Ninth Air Force's 'turf', Eighth Air Force leaders were intimately involved in planning the long-range, low-level, Ploesti mission – especially former 93rd BG boss, Col Ted Timberlake.

The B-24D Liberator was perhaps the only heavy bomber suitable for this mission. The D-model, the first version to see combat in the Eighth, and the only one in the frontline as of mid-1943, was powered by four 895-kW Pratt & Whitney R-1830 Twin Wasp turbocharged radial engines. It was credited with a maximum speed of 291 mph (467 km/h). On a practical mission, with a real-world fuel load, the B-24 could carry a greater bomb load than the B-17 – typically 8000 lb (3628 kg) vis-à-vis 6000 lb (2721 kg). It could also take any load farther, and fly faster. Alas, the B-24D model was not well-equipped with armour or defensive guns, however, but payload, speed and range were the qualities most needed in the attack on Ploesti, and the B-24D had them all.

The air forces' commander in the region, Maj Gen Lewis H Brereton, was in North Africa following horrific defeats in the Philippines in 1941 and Java in 1942 – he had been Gen Douglas MacArthur's air commander when Japan launched its attack, and had been largely prevented by MacArthur from using his bomber force effectively. Viewed as a lacklustre figure by many who served with him, Brereton was the 'brain' – or, in the view of some, the 'culprit' – behind the raid.

'I feel the surprise element will weigh heavily in our favour', he recalled later. 'It is necessary to insure the heaviest possible damage in the first attack. Because of the long distance involved, 2000 miles (3218 km), and the danger of bad weather, I feel that our formations might get dispersed and not hit the target so effectively from a high altitude as they would in a low-level attack'.

Yes, after studying the targets in and around Ploesti, it was Brereton who had decided on the low-level mission, and caused the upset of all those English cows. His final assessment before the raid was flown;

'We expect our losses to be 50 per cent, but even if we lose everything we've sent but hit the target, it will be worth it.'

Some 179 B-24s made up the *Tidal Wave*, which set forth from dust-strewn desert bases around Benghazi starting at 0400 on 1 August 1943. Those from the Eighth Air Force retained their olive-drab camouflage, while those belonging to the Ninth wore a sand-coloured scheme, 'Eightballs', 'Traveling Circus', 'Sky Scorpions', 'Liberandos'

A combination aircraft, automobile, and tractor en route to Berlin comprised the artist's rendering on the nose of B-24D-5-CO Liberator 41-23819 *RUGGED BUGGY*, which belonged to the 68th BS/44th BG. It was lost on the 14 May 1943 mission to Kiel (*via Will Lundy*)

B-24D-25-CO Liberator 41-24225 *FLAK ALLEY* boasted an athletic young woman attired in nothing but panties. Aside from this female form, five swastikas below its mission tally denoted that the combined claims of the aircraft's gunners made this bomber an ace. Belonging to the 68th BS/44th BG, *FLAK ALLEY* was lost in action on 24 February 1944 (*via Will Lundy*)

and 'Pyramiders' vaulted skyward, at last putting to work all of that low-level training.

One aircraft crashed on take-off, another flew into the sea, and the lead B-24 was attacked by a Bf 109, forcing it to jettison its bombs early and crash. Finally, no fewer than ten Liberators had to abort and return to base, their engines fouled by the persistent sand.

The strike force was to head north to Corfu, then swing to the north-east. At Corfu, the lead bomber, B-24D-120-CO 42-40563 *WONGO-WONGO* of the 512th BS/376th BG, piloted by 1Lt Brian Flavelle, inexplicably began pitching violently. With the mission navigator, Capt Robert F Wilson, on board, this Liberator stood abruptly on its tail in mid-air. It shuddered, then dived suddenly straight into the sea. Radio silence was being observed, and no one knew what had happened. *WONGO-WONGO's* wingman went down to investigate, found no sign of survivors, and ultimately had to abort and return to North Africa, carrying the deputy mission navigator.

On approach to the target, the 376th BG mistook the IP (initial point) at Floresti and turned south too soon. The 93rd BG followed but, thanks to second-thinking and prompt action by pilot Lt Col. Addison Baker and co-pilot Maj John L Jerstad in B-24D-120-CO 42-40994 *HELL'S WENCH* of the 328th BS, the group made another turn which took it back in the direction of Ploesti. Among the trailing groups, the 389th flew north-east toward its target at Campina, 17 miles (27 km) north of the main refinery. Some confusion persisted as the 44th and 98th BGs pressed on, but both reached the correct IP at Floresti and proceeded to their assigned targets. Over the target, navigational mix-ups caused some of the refineries to be attacked by too many Liberators, and others by two few. Dodging fighters and flak, many of the bombers flew into cables raised as barriers in their path by balloons.

Flying at low level, in gusting turbulence, confronting enemy fighters and gunfire . . . no one could doubt the courage of Liberator crews who went against Ploesti, but decades later one of them would 'foam at the mouth' when the mission was included in a book about famous military blunders. In war, success requires risk. The Ploesti attackers were going into nothing less than a fiery furnace.

HEROIC ACTIONS

In the midst of the inferno, the B-24 Liberator crews displayed incredible heroism. Hit by an 88 mm shell and several mortar rounds, Baker and Jerstad in *HELL'S WENCH* could have belly-landed in an open field, but instead rushed at Ploesti's smoke stacks, trailing flames. The 389th BG had nine B-24s from a sixteen-ship formation destroyed, proving its share of losses to be even worse than Brereton had predicted. Nevertheless, CO, Col Jack Wood, pressed home his attack despite a wall of gunfire.

A few Liberator crew members had undergone an unexpected change of assignment before the mission. For example, co-pilot 2Lt Deane Cavit had travelled to North Africa with the 567th BS/389th BG, only to be told that he and his crew were transferring to the 343rd BS/98th BG. Cavit believes that about a dozen crews were so affected, but that most came from the 'Eightballs' or the 'Circus', rather than the 'Sky Scorpions'. If so, he may be one of the very few Eighth Air Force Liberator crew member who never flew a mission in the Eighth Air Force!

'Our element started out with eight aircraft', he remembers. 'Five of them reached the target and all five were shot down. Only two of us got out of my plane'. Cavit was one of 110 men who survived bailouts over the Ploesti area, most of whom spent 13 months in a prison camp in Romania, and were then liberated by friendly troops.

Despite potent defences and heavy losses, the Ploesti bombing succeeded in inflicting damage on major portions of the Romanian oil fields-although some of the intended targets escaped unscathed.

Liberators fought sluggishly through those demented skies over Romania, and struggled to make it home. One sign of the level of difficulty of this mission was that the number of people killed on the ground was apparently no greater than the number who died in the air.

The final results showed that 179 Liberators took off, 14 aborted and 165 attacked. Of the B-24 losses, 33 were to flak and 10 to fighters. Fifty-six Liberators were damaged, and eight aircraft recovered in Turkey. Of those B-24s which returned to North Africa, 99 recovered at their originating bases, while the remaining 15 landed elsewhere. 532 aviators died.

It would forever be debated how these bombings affected Germany's ability to fuel its combat forces, but no one doubted that a mighty blow had been dealt to the Reich. Baker, Jerstad, Johnson and 2Lt Lloyd H Hughes, the pilot of B-24D 42-40753 (564th BS/389th BG), were all awarded the Medal of Honor, with all but Leon Johnson's being posthumous. A fifth Medal of Honor went to the Ninth Air Force's Col Kane.

After Ploesti, the 'detached' Liberator groups from the Eighth

Joseph McConnell was a B-24 navigator with the 448th BG, flying from Seething, in Norfolk (Station 146) in 1943-44. In postwar years, he became a pilot, and went on to shoot down sixteen enemy aircraft in Korea to become the top American air ace of the 1950-53 conflict – this photo shows him during the Korean War (*via Robert F Dorr*)

It was always good news for a group's lead bombardier when explosions were bunched together at the centre of a target. The significance of the daylight bombing campaign has been debated, but there is no doubt that Allied heavy bombers were a major irritant to the German war machine. This is an attack on the Zahnradfabrick Works at Freidrichshafen, which was one of the largest gear-cutting factories in the world. The results shown are a mix of explosive and incendiary detonations (*via John Stanaway*)

Seen much later in the Vietnam era, George S Brown commanded the 93rd BG's 329th BS as a lieutnant colonel. When the rest of the 93rd went to North Africa for the winter of 1942-43, Brown remained in England with his unit. On 2 January 1943, four 329th Liberators, including one flown by Brown, made the first ever penetration of German airspace by AAF bombers (*USAF*)

flew four post-*Husky* missions, to Wiener Neustadt on 13 August, to Foggia, Italy, on 16 and 18 August and to the Cancello depot and marshalling yards on 21 August. During their sojourn in the Mediterranean, Eighth groups had launched 990 sorties and lost 54 bombers. Their gunners claimed 121 enemy aircraft destroyed. Aside from the Ploesti dead, a further 35 men had been killed in other actions, and many others wounded or captured. The Eighth Air Force's Liberators were still completing their North African stay on 17 August 1943 when B-17 Flying Fortresses from bases in England undertook the infamous Schweinfurt-Regensburg mission in which 60 heavy bombers were lost.

AUTUMN 1943

For months to come, Ploesti would stand as the 'high water mark' for Liberator operations in Europe. Indeed, early sorties over the continent had produced mixed results at best, and there was grounds to believe that German defences would grow stronger, not weaken. The Bf 109 (which Americans always called the 'ME 109') and the Fw 190 were now painfully familiar to Liberator crews, as were the much-respected German 88 mm anti-aircraft guns or flak, which comes from the German word for aircraft defence gun, *fliegerabwherkanone*.

As the war progressed, the Germans would begin to encircle crucial targets with as many as 40 heavy guns of various calibres in what they called a *grossbatterie*, creating two rings of these monster weapons, and using radar to alert them of when the bombers were coming.

Radar, it seemed, was the Achilles Heel in the otherwise formidable Reich defences, for Germany lagged far behind the Allies in its development. Indeed, the *Würzburg* aircraft tracking system fell far short of the state of the art as the war progressed. As for the infamous '88', guns of this calibre made up about 75 per cent of the heavy flak weapons ranged against the Allies, yet only the late-arriving 88/41 was regarded as effective against targets flying above 26,000 ft (7300 m).

In the autumn of 1943, the B-24D Liberator was still inadequately armed, especially when it came to dealing with the frontal attacks in which the Luftwaffe had begun to specialise. Friendly fighter escort was still only a part-reality, 'sort of like kissing your sister', as one crew member put it. The lack of replacements for both aircraft and crews prevented the mounting of B-24 missions of adequate size, and it was not until the late 1943 that the Liberator began 'earning its keep' in the Eighth.

The 392nd BG made its combat debut on 9 September 1943, and it would go on to participate in 285 missions by the time Liberators ceased dropping their lethal payloads on 25 April 1945. Dubbed the 'Crusaders', the group made its debut with olive-drab B-24Hs wearing the letter 'D' in an enclosed circle – the group had the distinction of being the first combat group equipped with H-models assigned to the Eighth Air Force.

Development of the B-24H was direct result of the D-model's vulnerability to head-on attacks by Luftwaffe fighters. Ford and Emerson worked together to adapt a power turret, originally designed as a tail turret installation, to be used in the nose of the bomber. Installation of the Emerson A-15 in the nose required no fewer than 56 engineering changes to the earlier B-24D airframe. The addition of the turret increased length of the B-24H to 67 ft 3 $^{3}/_{16}$ in (20.50 m), or about a foot more than the B-24D.

To accommodate the 190 lb (86.18 kg) weight increase that came hand-in-glove with the new turret installation, engineers had to redesign the bombardier's station and change the nose landing gear doors from inward- to downward-opening. Pilots welcomed an aircraft with an altered centre of gravity that was no longer tail-heavy, and no longer prone to cruising in a nose-up attitude that one critic called 'snooty'. The first B-24H (42-7465) was delivered from the Ford Willow Run facility on 20 June 1943,

The B-24H model also introduced an improved Consolidated A-6B tail turret with larger Plexiglas panels on both sides, giving the gunner enhanced visibility, plus a few other minor improvements. Perhaps no other aircraft so dramatically symbolised how the Axis was outmatched by the American industrial machine, for Ford could not only produce a complete B-24H every 56 minutes, but also construct major portions of two more bombers in that same period.

To handle this prodigious output, the latter were completed as 'knock-down' kits, and transported overland, or by rail, to Consolidated, in Fort Worth, and Douglas, in Tulsa, for final assembly. When travelling by road, the incomplete Liberator used up two-and-a-half special trailers, 84 of which were eventually constructed solely for this purpose. At 63 ft (19.50 m) in length, and handled by two drivers who 'spelled' each other every five hours, the trailers were among the largest vehicles on the two-lane

The control tower of the 448th BG at Seething, in Norfolk, (alias Station 146) was typical of the facilities available to Eighth Air Force members. It was simply a concrete block building with an enclosed structure at the top (*Dale Van Blair*)

Seen here in typical enlisted Class 'A' uniform, Sgt Albert 'Shorty' Spadafore was a ball turret gunner in the 715th BS/448th BG. He arrived in England in late 1943, and after several successful missions with his regular crew in late 1943 and early 1944, Spadafore filled in with a different crew when *TWIN TAILS* (San Diego-built B-24D-70-CO Liberator 42-100122) set forth on an 8 March 1944 strike. After being damaged by smoke bombs dropped by the PFF ship leading the formation, *TWIN TAILS* lost fuel and had to ditch in the English Channel 25 miles (40 km) east of Great Yarmouth. Spadafore was not among the two men who survived the impact when the Liberator broke up during the rough water landing (*Dale Van Blair*)

highways of America.

The B-24H was soon followed by the B-24J. Both had a ball turret which could be retracted into the fuselage when not in use. The B-24H and B-24J had different nose turrets, bombsights, and autopilots, and a different shape to the bombardier's transparency, but they enjoyed similarities in performance and capability. So too did the B-24L, with its new lightweight tail gun position replacing a powered turret (and its ready suitability as a *Mickey* aircraft, carrying the H2X PFF, or pathfinder, radar), and the B-24M, which reverted to the standard tail turret.

The H-, J-, L- or M-model Liberator could launch from a base in England, fly 830 miles (1335 km), drop a bombload of up to 20,000 lb (9071 kg) and make the return trip while defending itself with considerable tenacity from ever more persistent Luftwaffe fighters. For its longest missions of over 1000 miles (1610 km), the Liberator carried a much-reduced bombload of 6000 lb (2721 kg), which usually consisted of a dozen 500-lb (227-kg) bombs.

Long after it introduced the B-24H and went into action, the 392nd BG acquired new markings from May 1944, with a black horizontal bar applied over all-white stabilisers. Led at first by Col Irvine A Randle, the

B-24Ds form up into their pre-briefed flights of three whilst cruising over East Anglia prior to setting off for 'Fortress Europe'. This photo was taken in late 1943 (*Kent Jaquith*)

392nd flew from Wendling (Station 118), in Norfolk. In time, its squadrons wore the following codes: 576th BS (CI), 577th BS (DC), 578th BS (EC) and 579th BS (GC). By war's end, the 392nd had graduated to a mix of natural-metal B-24J/L/Ms.

A unique Eighth Air Force unit was the 482nd BG, which entered combat on 20 August 1943 (commanded by Col Baskin R Lawrence Jr) from Alconbury. Equipped mostly with Flying Fortresses, the 482nd BG reported to various headquarters while pioneering the use of radar bombing devices in Europe. One of the group's squadrons, the 814th BS (coded SI) operated both B-17 and B-24 bombers on PFF, or radar-pathfinding missions.

OPERATION *STARKEY*

As a rehearsal for an eventual Allied invasion of the continent, Operation *Starkey* was launched in September 1943, and it brought the 44th, 93rd and 389th BGs back to the business of dropping bombs in Europe, together with the newly-arrived 392nd BG. The last-named group participated in a 6 September 1943 effort that sent 69 Liberators from the four groups against four targets in France.

The *Starkey* 'main event' came the next day, when a maximum effort saw 330 heavy bombers – accompanied by 144 B-26 Marauder medium bombers – hit targets a dozen targets scattered across France. Eighth Air Force planners had hoped to see how the Luftwaffe would react to such an armada, but the Germans refused to co-operate, and did not engage in significant numbers.

REORGANISATION

The heavy bomber component of the Eighth Air Force, namely VIII Bomber Command, underwent a shake-up on 13 September 1943. The higher headquarters that had been designated the 1st, 2nd and 4th Bomb Wings were redesignated the 1st, 2nd and 3rd Air Divisions. Of these, the 1st Air Division would remain all-B-17, the 2nd Air Division would remain all-B-24, and the 3rd Air Division would operate both heavy bombers, before becoming all-B-17.

The Eighth Air Force was a long way from the strength it would

Ford B-24H-1-FO Liberator 42-7478 of the 578th/392nd BG was photographed on a sortie from Wendling. Note the impressive double row of bomb tally mission markers forward of the cockpit (*Ken A McLean*)

While Eighth Air Force 'heavy' crews were pounding European targets in olive-drab Liberators with glass noses, American industry was gearing up to produce newer, natural-metal bombers with turrets up front. This Ford B-24H-25-FO Liberator (42-95051) represented an 'interim' step toward the eventual definitive version. Although Ford bombers would have enlarged waist-gun window positions, this particular bomber retained the earlier, smaller windows (*Consolidated*)

eventually reach, but in time its order of battle would include the following: for the 1st Air Division, 12 bomb groups in four wings; for the 2nd Air Division, 14 bomb groups (all-B-24) in five wings, and for the 3rd Air Division also, 14 bomb groups in five wings. Each numbered air force would also possess, in time, a fighter wing equipped with five groups.

As airfields continued to be constructed, and bombers continued to arrive from the US, the tempo of operations over Europe increased. Between 8-14 October 1943, Eighth Air Force bomber crews went into action in what became the horrendous 'Black Week' in which 148 heavy bombers were lost on just four missions – 143 of these were Flying Fortresses, with just five Liberators included among the casualties. In the latter two of the four missions, Liberators flew diversionary raids while Flying Fortresses went against heavily-defended targets at Munster and Schweinfurt. 'Black Week' was the evidence needed by leaders of the Allied Bomber Offensive that more, and better, fighters were needed to escort the bombers to their objectives.

The 445th BG began combat on 13 December 1943. Commanded at first by Col Robert H Terrill, and assigned to Tibenham (Station 124), in Norfolk, the 445th comprised the 700th BS (eventually to be coded RN), the 701st BS (MK), the 702nd BS (WV) and the 703rd BS (IS). The group would eventually fly 282 missions, consisting of 7145 sorties dropping 16,732 tons of bombs, and would win the dubious distinction of losing more Liberators on a single raid than any other outfit – 30 bombers on 27 September 1944.

This B-24H of the 44th BG barely made it home to Shipdham following a mission over Occupied Europe on 18 November 1943. Its pilot on this occasion was Lt Rockford Griffths (*Norman Taylor*)

Opposite page
Because there were two Liberators nicknamed *THE frightful OLD PIG* during the war, it is unclear which bomb group operated this particular example (Fort Worth-built B-24J-10-CF 42-64257). The carefully-applied artwork is typical of the painting expertise of men at embarkation points such as Grenier Army Air Field, New Hampshire, who created 'nose-art' for crews heading to war. Note how the artwork has increased dramatically in size in the top photo when compared with the lower view. By the time 1943 ended, the number of Liberators heading toward Eighth Air Force bases was growing into a crowd. Many did not retain the artwork applied stateside (*Norman Taylor*)

This group is remembered by some because Hollywood actor James Stewart commanded the 700th BS, before transferring later to the 453rd BG group staff. The 445th BG remained in combat until 25 April 1945, making the transition from olive-drab to natural metal.

Stewart's contribution to the war effort has often been overlooked. When he died in 1997, most news reports, including one from the US Air Force's own news bureau, credited him with flying B-17 Flying Fortresses in combat – a low blow, in the opinion of Liberator men. Other stories linked him with Hollywood stars who wore uniforms but did not have serious military duties, like Ronald Reagan and Clark Gable.

The truth was that Stewart flew B-24s, and he was more than a 'celebrity in uniform'. Stewart was very much a combat pilot, officer and leader. One veteran of the 445th BG remembers that 'we couldn't keep him out of the cockpit', and 'the brass were worried about what might happen to such a well-known figure'.

Stewart briefly commanded the 703rd BS, but was 'bucked up' to group headquarters where the brass hoped he would keep his feet on the ground. Instead, he flew missions as air commander. 'No question about his wanting to get into it with "both hands"', one veteran recalls. Eventually, Stewart was transferred to the 453rd BG to work for another of the war's genuine Liberator heroes, Ramsay Potts.

The 446th BG joined the fray on 16 December 1943, operating from Bungay (Station 125), in Suffolk, hence the nickname 'Bungay Buckaroos'. This group initially operated B-24H models, and later J-, L- and M-models. The first commander of the 'Buckaroos' was Col Jacob J Brogger, and his squadrons were the 704th BS (later to be coded FL/red), 705th BS (HN/yellow), 706th BS (RT/ white) and the 707th BS (JU/blue). Ultimately, the 446th BG would complete 273 missions and fly 7259 sorties by 25 April 1945. One of this group's bombers, B-24H-1-CF 41-29144 *RONNIE* of the 704th BS is believed to have been the first Eighth Air Force Liberator to complete 200 missions, although this has been much debated over the years.

The final B-24 combat group to enter the war in 1943 was the 448th BG, which undertook its first mission on 22 December 1943. Initially

commanded by Col James M Thompson, the 448th operated from Seething (Station 146), in Norfolk. Ultimately, the 448th would complete 262 missions and 6774 sorties. The group's squadrons (and their subsequent codes) were the 712th BS (CT), 713th BS (IG), 714th BS (EI) and 715th BS (IO).

For everyday utility needs, all bomb groups had 'hack' aircraft in addition to their Liberators, and it seems that the 448th BG may have had more than others. At various times, it possessed an Airspeed Oxford (with hand brakes that puzzled Liberator pilots accustomed to foot brakes), an ex-French Douglas DB-7 similar to the AAF's A-20 Havoc, a P-47 Thunderbolt with shark's teeth, which was used by group officers to 'ride herd' on Liberator formations, and a Noorduyn UC-64 Norseman, the same airframe in which renowned band leader Glenn Miller later perished.

Among members of the 448th BG was a Liberator navigator by the name of 1Lt Joseph S McConnell. In his postwar career, McConnell became a pilot and, at the controls of the F-86 Sabre, ended up as the American 'ace of aces' during the 1950-53 Korean War (see *Osprey Aircraft of the Aces 4 - Korean War Aces* for further details). When Hollywood wrapped its version of his life, entitled *The McConnell Story*, starring Alan Ladd and June Allyson, the film placed McConnell aboard a B-17 Flying Fortress – yet another slight of the kind Liberator crew members were to experience all their lives.

One pilot who went to England with the 448th BG (after the group had begun operations) was Edward K 'King' Schultz Jr. Along with about 20 other Liberator crews, he and his men made their final stop in the US at Grenier Army Airfield in Manchester, New Hampshire, before heading eastbound to the UK. At Grenier, Schultz encountered a sergeant who offered to paint a beautiful caricature on the nose of his Liberator in exchange for a handsome fee.

Schultz and his crew scrounged up the princely sum of $40, which was more than they could afford, for a very personalised rendering on B-24H-20-DT 41-29000. What the sergeant may have known, and Schultz didn't, was that immediately upon arrival in England, the Liberator was snatched away from Schultz and his crew!

'Aircraft newly-arrived in Europe were sent to depot to be modified for combat', 'King' later lamented. That usually meant that they were despatched to Burtonwood, in Lancashire, where armoured plate was added beside the pilot and co-pilot positions – more often than not, olive-drab armour plate on an aircraft that was otherwise natural aluminium. Schultz never saw the Liberator with his personal art on it again. The effort by the paintbrush virtuoso at Grenier Field had been in vain.

FIGHTERS

In October and November 1943, Luftwaffe fighter resistance seemed unpredictable, but they were always on the minds of Liberator gunners, who believed that there was a special yellow-nosed outfit at Abbeville containing 'hotshot' pilots. Sgt M P Curphey, top turret gunner on a Liberator of the 564th BS/389th BG remembers;

'We were told they had "hotshots" at Abbeville. Approaching our target, I saw some yellow-nosed '109s coming in on us. Somebody called out "pea shooters in target area". When I looked out across numbers' three and four engines, I could see a few '109s bouncing along just out of range. I wondered if they could be the "hotshots" we were told we might sometimes encounter. The little "pea shooters" were climbing as they passed us by. We didn't have long to wait to verify their status. As we were leading an element, we were the first to be attacked.

'This Messerschmitt came in from 12 O'Clock high. Twelve "fifties" converged on him. The tracers were visible bouncing off his spinner and probably his wind screen. At the last moment he gave us a three- or four-second burst of cannon fire. We were flying a very tight formation, yet this "hotshot" was able to flip onto his side and slip through our formation, diving as he did so. Our ball turrets pounded ".50s" into his belly. You could see the tracers skipping off. Although we received five or six hits, we received no disabling damage or serious injury. The second and third '109s hit the ships on our wings. They went down, as did the ship on our tail. No German planes damaged as far as I could see. We kept

This Liberator of the 704th BS/446th BG was photographed travelling through flak over Europe (*via Clyde Gerdes*)

thinking about what Maj Gen Curtis LeMay (3rd Bomb Division) had told us, "Gentlemen you are being paid to put bombs on the target. There will be NO evasive action between the IP and the target".'

In December 1943 Liberators went to Bremen, Emden, Osanbruck and Munster. They also began operations against sites near the Pas de Calais, where the Germans were said to be readying some kind of secret weapon. No one knew, yet, what the weapon might be. It was rumoured that the Germans had a jet-powered robot bomb, or a rocket. In one barracks where crew members bantered, it was said they were developing a time machine. Whatever it was, no fewer than 722 heavy bombers went there on Christmas Eve.

Although two 448th BG bombers collided over the target and limped home mortally damaged, it was a remarkable achievement. A year earlier, the idea of putting 700 heavy bombers into the air had been only a dream. In the final mission of the year, another 572 'heavies' were put aloft.

In Berlin, Hitler's armaments expert Albert Speer predicted that the Third Reich would be in trouble if the Allied Bombing Offensive directed its attentions to the ball-bearing industry, or to aircraft construction plants, on any kind of sustained basis. He probably did not know how right he was. By now, German leaders were openly debating the obvious – that the Allies were preparing to invade the continent. As for the Liberator force in Europe, it now consisted of seven combat groups (44th, 93rd, 389th, 392nd, 445th, 446th and the 448th BGs), and it was still growing. In the months to come, its size would triple.

1944

Like a great tree growing from a tiny acorn, the Eighth Air Force, by January 1944, had expanded to a size and shape beyond the vision of all but the greatest of optimists who had brought American air power to England's shores two years earlier.

Charged with conducting the daylight strategic air campaign over Europe (in conjunction with the newly-formed Fifteenth Air Force in the Mediterranean) while the Royal Air Force bombed at night, the 'Mighty Eighth' was growing toward its ultimate strength of three air divisions and seven combat wings, each comprising three to five combat groups. In the past 12 months alone, the number of B-24 groups had built to seven, with five additional B-17 groups joining the growing Eighth, and as the new year began, many were training relentlessly by 'bombing' English villages and friendly installations.

For every group, there had to be an airfield. Here, American and British allies worked together to carve runways, taxyways and revetments out of tough topsoil that was often a quagmire of clawing mud. Some Liberator crews lived briefly in tents but most Americans were soon the beneficiaries of a vast network of barracks, mess halls, recreation facilities, maintenance buildings and administrative structures.

Ambitions were high. Air power would become the decisive force over the continent. But reality conflicted with ambition, and England was socked in. Throughout much of January and February, on most days Liberator crews saw little but fog, rain and murk. There were exceptions: 569 'heavies' were despatched to the harbour facilities at Kiel on 4 January 1944, of which 486 reached the target. Six Liberators were lost in combat and one diverted to the safe haven of Sweden. Some 245 bombers were sent to Kiel the following day, of which 225 delivered their warloads and five B-24s were lost.

Horace S 'Hal' Turell of the 703rd BS/445th BG described the second trip to Kiel in a quote which stresses the role of the navigator on a combat sortie;

'It was my crew's fifth mission. The bomb load for our group comprised thermite incendiaries. These are stick-like bombs about 36

The 489th BG joined the fight on the eve of the Allied landings in Normandy. In this shot, taken from the group's assembly ship *L'IL COOKIE* (Ford-built B-24E-FO 42-7552) apparently on 5 July 1944, *The Sharon D.* (Ford-built B-24H-15-FO Liberator 42-94759, assigned to the group's deputy commander, Lt Col Leon Vance, who was already being recommended for the Medal of Honor) and *"PHONEY EXPRESS"* (Ford-built B-24H-20-FO 42-94833 of the 844th BS) are seen joining up over England in preparation for a mission to the Continent (*Charles Frudenthal*)

Jo, normally flown by 2Lt Frank Elston of the 489th BG, was Ford-built B-24H 42-94783. For reasons lost to antiquity, Elston was slower than his contemporaries in winning the boost to first lieutenant that became virtually automatic during the war years, so he boasted of having an 'oak leaf cluster' to his second lieutenant's bars – a non-existent insignia of rank. The yellow tail indicates that this photo was taken after the 489th BG had joined the 20th BW in mid-August 1944 (*Charles Frudenthal*)

inches long and about one inch in diameter, loaded with thermite. They were in bundles that opened on release to scatter over a wide area of a city.

'On the bomb run we lost oil pressure in number three engine and had to feather it. We were able to stay with the group through the bomb run. The deputy lead had not dropped its bombs, so the group made another bomb run. Because of traffic the group climbed 1500 ft (4572 m). With one engine out we could not keep up.

'We stayed with the group about 1500 ft (4572 m) below them. I was the navigator. I looked up through my astro hatch and saw a B-24 with its bomb bay doors open directly above us. I called this out to the pilot and he immediately turned away just as the bombs came down. Two struck our airplane and bounced off. A third stuck in the wing right in the gas tank for No 3 engine. It did not go off. We were now hopelessly separated from the group.

'At this point two ME 109s made firing passes across our nose from 10 o'clock high. Two Ju 88s finished off another B-24 behind us and headed for us. The pilot put the plane into a power dive and skidded it at the same time. My airspeed needle went to the stops. We made it into cloud cover about 4000 ft (12,192 m) below and disappeared from the Germans' view. They no doubt argued as to who had gotten us. At the moment of the dive I got a good landmark fix, so when in the clouds I gave the pilot a course for base.

'If you look at the map of Germany you will see that this portion of north Germany extends like a boxing glove to the North Sea. A straight course home would have taken us back over Germany, and their radar flak. Also, we never knew when the cloud cover would run out. I had plotted a dog leg around Germany that brought us in over Scotland. We had plenty of gas, so that was not a problem. The pilot went back to check our damage and I got busy calculating our turns and ETA.

'I looked at the compass and noted we were flying 45 degress left of my plotted course, and that the radio compass was on and pointed to zero. Obviously the co-pilot had turned it on and was homing in on our base. I exploded in anger, as I did not know how long he had been doing this, and it ruined my dead reckoning, which was all we had to go by.

Capt Bob Gordon, a navigator with the 489th BG, braces in front of the famous *The Sharon D.*, which kept this nickname throughout the war, even though the pilot who assigned the name only flew two missions in it, and was in a different Liberator when he earned the Medal of Honor. The aircraft survived to be scrapped after the war (*Charles Frudenthal*)

They all had a picture like this, and they all looked so young and fresh when they arrived, but flak, fighters, and freezing temperatures at altitude all conspired to make them older men all too quickly. 1Lt John A Jakab of the 787th BS/466th BG (back row, far right) poses with his crew in February 1944, just after they flew Ford-built B-24H Liberator 42-52610 from their training base in the US to their wartime base at Attlebridge, near Norwich. Gunner S/Sgt Arthur R Kelly (front row, far right) typifies the 'All American look' of these young men who arrived in England bristling with confidence and quickly acquired a better appreciation of real life. Jakab remembers that the aircraft was nicknamed *THE MADAME*, 'and the name had been printed on the side in chalk by my engineer (S/Sgt Elmer C Umholtz, front row, centre). We had intended to have the name painted on by an artist in the group, but the ship was lost in combat with another crew before this could be accomplished' *(John Jakab)*

'I called him and said if he wanted a course for Germany I could give him a shorter one, and I would bail out as soon as we were over land. Obviously others were listening, and the pilot came on and ordered the co-pilot to get back on the course I had given. He then crawled through the tunnel to my office to see what I was up to. He agreed and went back to his seat. I applied some Kentucky windage to my calculations, and we came out of the overcast right over our base. Now the question was do we try to land this thing?

'The pilot gave everyone a choice of bailing out. He said he thought he could bring it in. We all elected to stay with the ship. That was the smoothest, softest, landing Ralph ever made. As soon as the plane stopped we all scattered. The armament officer pulled the bomb out and set it down on the field. He then took a shot at it and it went off! Interestingly the terror was quite varied depending on the position. The pilot and I were too busy to be scared. The engineer told me he sat in the top turret staring at that bomb the entire time just frozen. The tail gunner could not see it, nor could the bombardier in the nose and ball turrets. The waist gunners who could see it were also paralysed as, obviously, was the co-pilot. After landing I shook for a long time.'

On 7 January, 502 bombers were sent and 420 arrived over Ludwigshaven – 120 B-24s had launched as part of this mission, but only 69 had managed to drop bombs. The 44th BG was recalled whilst over the North Sea off Cromer, on the north Norfolk coast.

Frankfurt was the objective on 29 January, when 188 Liberators climbed out of soupy England for a long haul through flak and fighters. Five B-24s were lost. 143 Liberators went to Hanover a few days later and two were lost.

ENTER THE 453rd

The weather was grounding everything, including the birds, when the 453rd BG arrived on 5 February 1944. On that day, the 2nd Air Division mounted a mission to Tours. It was plagued by weather problems. The next day, with the newly-arrived 453rd BG participating again, weather forced the recall of 250 B-24s after their launch. This became an incredible mess, with hundreds of men struggling to bring criss-crossing sections of Liberators safely down through the clouds to earth. Incredibly, there were no collisions.

As for the 453rd BG, it reported to the 2nd Combat Bomb Wing (CBW), 2nd Air Division. Commanded at first by Col Joseph A Miller, who was eventually lost on a mission, the group flew from Old Buckenham (Station 144), in Norfolk, initially with B-24H models. In the latter part of his European tour, actor James Stewart served on the 453rd BG staff.

The group's flying units were the 732nd BS (eventually to be coded E3), 733rd BS (F8), 734th BS (E8) and 735th BS (H6). The group eventually operated B-24J/L/Ms, and flew 259 missions, making up 6655 sorties, before being withdrawn on 12 April 1945. But in February 1944, these men were the 'new kids on the block', and most of them wondered how they could inflict any air power on anybody in the weather that clung to them like a disease.

On 10 February 1944 the 448th BG sent 26 Liberators to attack Rijen airfield in Holland, and the very real fog in the English air combined with the figurative 'fog' of war. Two Liberators aborted with instrument malfunctions. Then one B-24 flew into another, ripping it in two, becoming entangled with it, and plunging to the ground. Of 20 men aboard the two bombers, only two were thrown free and able to parachute safely. The results over the target were unclear at best, and a grim mood hung over the 448th as it flew further missions that month and the next, some of them *Noball* sorties against the sites where Germany was developing its V1 flying bomb.

Noball was the Eighth Air force code word for the missions aimed at countering the pulsejet-powered cruise missile known to Americans as a 'buzz bomb'. Navigator Hal Turell remembers that;

'The first few were literally "milk runs". Then the Germans hardened the V1 sites with "88s". To even out the odds, we went in at lower altitudes. For me, most of them were at 10,000 to 12,000 ft (3048 to 3658 m). The Germans had remarkably good aim.'

Many of the Americans knew little or nothing about the secret weapons being developed by the Reich, but referred to the V1 installations (not quite accurately) as the 'rocket coast'.

In February, March and April of 1944, more than two-dozen important missions were mounted by B-24 crews of the Eighth. The largest number of missions (though not of sorties, since other missions used more aircraft) were directed at V1 sites. Some of the targets were also the first V2 installations, where a true ballistic rocket was being aimed as a terror weapon against England.

NEW ORGANISATION

15 February 1944 was the official start-up date for a reorganisation that began in practical terms at the

Lt Col Leon R Vance Jr arrived in England in May 1944 as deputy commander of the 489th BG. On his second mission, on the eve of the D-Day landings in Normandy, Vance was functioning as group commander when his Ford-built B-24H Liberator was smashed by flak explosions, killing the pilot and leaving the co-pilot seriously injured. Despite suffering grave wounds himself, Vance took control of the aircraft and made a desperate attempt to save others in the crew during a perilous ditching in the English Channel. He subsequently won a Medal of Honor for his efforts (*USAF*)

The goal of putting huge daylight bombing formations over the Third Reich required the best leaders. But decades later, Liberator veterans would still be arguing among themselves as to whether they received as much attention as men like the commander of the B-17 Flying Fortress-equipped 91st BG at Bassingborn, shown here beside Gen Dwight D Eisenhower. The third and final commander of Eighth Air Force, Lt Gen James Doolittle, is seen standing fourth from left in the front row of this group, which, according to the wartime caption, is examining a 1000-lb (454-kg) bomb. Did 'Ike 'and the others pay as much attention to B-24 Liberator crews as those flying the more readily recognised B-17? Today, opinions differ (*via Norman Taylor*)

Lt Gen James Doolittle (left) took command of the Eighth Air Force on 6 January 1944, and immediately freed up his fighter squadrons to use more aggressive tactics against the Luftwaffe – a decision that gave Flying Fortress and Liberator crews a better chance of survival. Gen Henry H 'Hap' Arnold (right) was the head of Army Air Forces (AAF), and an advocate of strategic air power. Doolittle, who held the Medal of Honor for the April 1942 B-25 Mitchell raid on Tokyo, ended his career at three-star rank, but was advanced to general on the retired list. Arnold was later one of the handful to achieve five-star rank, known at the time as 'general of the army'. In later years the term was retroactively changed to make Arnold the only 'general of the Air Force', ever (*via Norman Taylor*)

start of the year. Out went VIII Bomber Command, which had overseen the three heavy air divisions of the Eighth. Now that the Fifteenth Air Force had been established in the Mediterranean, an overall headquarters to co-ordinate the US bombing campaign over Europe was regarded as necessary.

Ultimately known as USSTAF (United States Strategic Air Forces), the new headquarters moved into the former Eighth billet at Bushey Park, and a new home for the Eighth Air Force was established at High Wycombe. Gen Carl 'Tooey' Spaatz returned to command USSTAF, and brought with him fabled air racer and Tokyo 'raider', Lt Gen James H 'Jimmy' Doolittle.

Replacement of Lt Gen Ira Eaker by Doolittle as commander of the Eighth Air Force was an unpopular move among Liberator men. In an 'eyes only' message to Spaatz, written in the telegraphic shorthand of the era, Eaker had argued, 'Believe war interest best served by my retention command Eighth Air Force. Otherwise experience this theatre for nearly two years wasted. If I am to be allowed, my personal preference having started with the Eighth and seen it organised for major tasks in this theater, it would be heartbreaking to leave just before climax. If my service satisfactory to seniors, request I be allowed to retain command Eighth Air Force'.

'If not', argued Eaker, 'command should go to Maj Gen Idwal H Edwards while', as Eaker saw it, 'Doolittle should head up Fifteenth'. None of his arguments were accepted.

To the end of their days, Doolittle and Eaker, who had known each other since the 1920s, addressed each other as 'General', rather than by first name. Eaker was shifted out of his job and replaced by Doolittle due to military politics, which wasn't really Doolittle's fault. Although Eisenhower was not particularly fond of Doolittle, the British General Sir Harold Alexander was, and he recommended that the same staff that had been in charge of the North African campaign should be brought back to England to run the war for the invasion of the continent. Doolittle was brought in and given command of the new Eighth Air Force (in essence, the former VIII Bomber Command), while Eaker was 'bumped up' and sent to the Mediterranean as the senior air officer.

Doolittle did not like the Liberator, and wanted to turn the Eighth Air Force into an all-B-17 force. Doolittle's main objections seem to be that the B-24 had become too heavy to reach the high altitudes needed to avoid the heavy flak over Germany. Granted, B-17s could operate at higher altitudes than the B-24s, but this argument overlooked the fact that the B-24 could carry more, fly faster and go farther.

Doolittle felt fighters should be used to destroy the Luftwaffe, rather than undertake exclusive close bomber escort. He visited Maj Gen William Kepner, VIII Fighter Command. On the wall of the office was the sign 'THE FIRST DUTY OF EIGHTH AIR FORCE FIGHTERS IS TO BRING THE BOMBERS BACK ALIVE'. When asked the origins of the sign, he was told it was there when Kepner arrived. Doolittle ordered another sign put up reading 'THE FIRST DUTY OF EIGHTH AIR FORCE FIGHTERS IS TO DESTROY GERMAN FIGHTERS'. He also ordered VIII Fighter Command to take the offensive.

This meant that while fighter formations did still provide close escort, they were also allowed to range ahead of the bombers and attack German fighter formations *before* they could assemble for co-ordinated and/or mass attacks against the bombers. Doolittle also allowed the fighters to strafe ground targets, including German airfields, in order to destroy the fighters on the ground. This was not a popular decision with bomber crews, who liked to see their 'little friends' nearby.

EUROPEAN CAMPAIGN

When the weather cleared over England, it turned miserable over the continent. While they gritted their teeth and awaited consistent flying weather, Liberator crews were being earmarked for an all-out effort as part of Operation *Argument*, the campaign against German aircraft manufacturing facilities which was deemed the top priority of the Allied bomber offensive. Better weather, and the all-out effort – to many, a turning point in the war – came during the six days of 20-25 February 1944.

The Eighth Air Force and the RAF put every airworthy four-engined bomber into the assault, and struck every major aircraft plant in the Third Reich on five of those six days.

'Big Week' started with the 20 February attack on Leipzig and the Tutow complex. That day, while frigid layers of cloud hung 500 ft (152 m) over much of England, and the temperature began to drop, 16 bomb groups of Liberators and Fortresses revved up their engines, strained against their brakes and awaited a command decision to risk the tricky English weather in the hope of reaching clear skies over the continent. The decision to launch the mission sent more than 1000 four-engined bombers roaring skyward. It was the first daylight bombing mission of its size, and for many B-24s, it was one of the longest at over nine hours.

AND THE 458th

The 458th BG entered combat on 22 February 1944 as part of the 96th CBW (which eventually included the 466th BG and 467th BG), 2nd Air Division. Located at Horsham St Faith (Station 119), in Norfolk, the 458th BG was initially commanded by Col James H Isbell. The group eventually flew 240 missions, racking up 5759 sorties. Its squadrons (and their eventual codes) were: 752nd BS (7V), 753rd BS (J4), 754th BS (Z5) and the 755th BS (J3). Among other achievements, the 458th carried out the first tests of the Azon bomb for the Eighth Air Force.

This weapon consisted of a finned unit bolted to a 1000-lb (454-kg) GP (general purpose) bomb. This transformed the Azon into a missile, which could be guided by the bombardier using a toggle switch that operated the fins. The Azon effort was led by Lt Col Robert W Vincent. Ten Liberators

Samuel E McGowan Snr was typical of the enlisted men who made up the bulk of B-24 Liberator flight crews. A member of the 328th BS/93rd BG, alias 'Ted's Travelling Circus', McGowan was an engineer and gunner. He flew on *NAUGHTY NAN* (B-24J-55-CO Liberator 42-99949, coded GO-I) and especially remembered his 11th mission against V-Bomb sites at Frederickschafen on 18 March 1944. 'I saw more enemy planes shot down on this mission than any other', he commented. 'The ground was white with a big snow, and they were easy to spot' (*Sam McGowan*)

The famous *The Sharon D.* cruises over spectacular cloud formations during a raid in September 1944 (*Charles Frudenthal*)

Liberators of the 489th BG at the release point over Cologne on 15 October 1944. What appears to be a blemish under the bomber farthest to the right is actually a burst of flak. The high aircraft in this image (second from right) is *TERRI ANN*, a Ford-Built B-24H-20-FO Liberator (42-94898, coded T4-B). The mix of olive-drab and natural-metal Liberators is typical for this juncture in the war (*Charles Frudenthal*)

were assigned to Azon duties and were fitted with radio antennas beneath the lower rear fuselage. The bomb was dropped from about 15,000 ft (6803 m), but only in clear weather, which was a rarity for Europe. 'More often than not', as George A. Reynolds, historian on the 458th, remembered later, 'crews were subjected to many alerts, only to have a last-minute "scrub" because of weather'.

Although the Azon bomb succeeded in the China-Burma-India Theater (to which these crews had been en route when the Eighth Air Force sought them for bridge and dock missions as D-Day approached), Reynolds saw it as 'a limited achievement' for the 458th, because only seven Azon sorties out of the total of thirteen were deemed to be successful. One of these was a 23 May 1944 mission by B-24H-10-CF (41-29300 *LORELEI* of the 753rd BS/458th BG, in which four Azon bombs 'dropped' four bridges, although no mention of the achievement ever reached official AAF records.

No fewer than seven of the ten Liberators assigned to Azon missions were eventually lost, most in landing mishaps. Azon crews designed, but never had time to manufacture or wear, an unofficial patch which identified them as the 'Buck Rogers Boys', named for the film-serial outer space hero adventurer of 1930s cinema fame.

6 March 1944 marked the first major Eighth Air Force mission to Berlin. Reichsmarschall Herman Göring, as head of the Luftwaffe, had predicted that Allied warplanes would never fly over the German capital. For B-17 Flying Fortress crews who made up the bulk of the strike, it was the costliest mission of the war. It was also painful for Liberator crews of the 2nd Air Division, whose primary target was the Daimler-Benz aero engine works in the suburb of Genshagen.

To attack this site, the combat groups of the 2nd Air Division sent a veritable armada. From this juncture onward, Liberator raids would often involve two or three combat wings, each contributing three or more combat groups, and the heavy bombers themselves would be measured not by the dozen, but by the hundred.

The 2nd Combat Wing sent the 445th, 453rd and 389th BGs into the target area in box after box totalling 61 Liberators, followed two minutes later by a composite force from the 14th and 96th Combat Wing comprising 61 more B-24s from the 392nd, 44th and 458th BGs. The final wave comprised 75 aircraft from the 20th Combat Wing's 446th,

It is almost impossible to see in this grainy snapshot, but Lt James A Struthers (67th BS/44th BG) and Lt M/Sgt Nelson are each holding a fifth of Scotch whisky (that is, one-fifth of a US gallon) to celebrate the incredible feat of 103 missions completed by *IRON CORSET*, alias Ford-built B-24H-30-FO 42-95318 (underline J). The occasion was also noteworthy because it was the 103rd mission performed by this bomber without an abort (early return), and also the 300th mission for the 44th BG in a period of 28 months. In addition to being marked with bomb silhouettes to signify missions completed, this Liberator wears five swastikas, making it an 'ace'. As for 'Curly' Nelson, he was an original combat engineer for the CO of the 67th BS, but he was eventually grounded with severe ear problems. He became a crew chief instead, and succeeded in compiling a most enviable tally of 129 missions with *IRON CORSET* without a single abort – this was a record within the 44th BG, and most other groups. The bomber was returned to the US in May 1945 and readied for the Pacific Theatre, but the call never came (*via Will Lundy*)

93rd and 448th BGs. The 482nd BG provided a single PFF (pathfinder) aircraft to lead each of these wing-sized formations.

Berlin was a triumph for long-ranged air power, but at the cost of fully one bomber out of every ten that set forth on the mission. The Eighth launched 814 bombers, 792 of which penetrated German territory – 69 were lost in battle. This staggering toll included 53 Fortresses and 16 Liberators, plus a P-38 Lightning, five P-47 Thunderbolts and five P-51 Mustangs – 229 Americans were killed, 411 taken prisoner and 40 diverted to Sweden, where they were interned.

The Allied Bomber Offensive now had the reach to strike at the heart of the Third Reich, and the fighters to accompany its bombers there, but the initial results were mixed: the total number of aircrew killed that day was almost identical to the number of Germans killed by falling bombs.

The B-24s reached Berlin after the 1st and 3rd Air Divisions with their B-17s. And although their losses were horrific, they were far closer to what the top brass could accept than the far heavier losses of the Flying Fortress groups.

REMINISCENCE

Dale Van Blair, a gunner with the 715th BS/448th BG, remembered going to the 'Big B' on 6 March 1944;

'I participated in the first mass daylight raid on Berlin. A few of those "other planes" (B-17s) had briefly hit the outskirts of the city on 3-4 March after ignoring a recall, but this was the first true mission to the capital. Although I normally flew in the tail turret, I was drafted to occupy the nose turret with another crew for this one. I knew the enlisted men of this crew but not the officers, and when I looked ahead at the flak barrage we were approaching, my main concern was whether the navigator or bombardier on this crew would take the time to let a stranger out of the nose turret if we had to bail out.

'I always left the doors of my tail turret open, thus I didn't have to depend on anyone to let me out. I couldn't do that, of course, in the nose turret. Fortunately, we made it through without any major damage. After that, I was ready to go back to my tail turret, where I didn't have to worry about the flak that I saw, since by the time I saw it, we were leaving it – out of sight, out of mind.'

There were Liberators that fell short of the target and others that ditched in the English Channel coming home from the German capital. B-24J-105-CO 42-109796 *BALLS OF FIRE* of the 445th BG, piloted by 1st Lt Norman Serklund, suffered an electrical failure in its number two engine and had to drop away from the main bomber stream and turn for home. Pounced upon by a fighter, it went down ten miles (16 km) north-east of Furstenau. Three of the crew were killed, the remainder taken prisoner. B-24J-205-CO 42-109832 *DE-ICER* of the 93rd BG, with 1Lt James Harris at the controls was hit by heavy bursts of flak and went down in Spandau district, Feldstrasse, with seven killed and three taken prisoner.

Surviving Liberators came home from Berlin, many wallowing through the sky trailing smoke. More than one crew member kissed the ground in England, the same wet, miserable, ground that often made flying conditions abominable. Exhausted, bloodied, hurt and harried, B-24 crews, like their cousins in B-17s, were hardly in a

Ford-built B-24H 42-95155, coded 8R-U+, of the 846th BS/489th BG on a mission over Europe from its Halesworth base, in Suffolk. Natural metal was becoming routine by late 1944 (*Charles Frudenthal*)

mood to celebrate, but they had hammered a nail into Hitler's coffin.

Up to now, the question had been whether American heavy bombers operating in daylight could get through the Germans' formidable defences with an attack that was credible and effective. After that first trip to Berlin, the question was whether the Germans could achieve credibility or effect in stopping them.

466th BOMB GROUP

When the 466th BG was training stateside, a contest yielded a $10 prize for M/Sgt Gerald A Dieffenbach, who suggested calling the group 'The Flying Deck', and naming each squadron after a suit in a deck of cards. The 784th BS, or red squadron, would be Clubs, the 785th BS (gold) Diamonds, the 786th (blue) Hearts and the 787th (white) Spades.

A squadron commander would be 'King', an exec 'Jack' and individual crews identified by the numbers in their suit. Thus, crew 715 would be the 'ten and five of spades' – the group nickname stuck but, unsurprisingly, the crew designations never went far.

On 22 March 1944, the 466th BG joined the fight in Europe, and after May 1944, when in combat, the squadrons were identified, respectively, by codes T9, 2U, U8 and 6L. The group waged its war from Attlebridge (Station 120) in East Anglia, near Norwich. The first commander of the 466th BG was Col Arthur J Pierce.

Referring to the 466th BG's first combat, Lt Col John H Woolnough describes a Liberator outfit prepping for a mission;

'On the afternoon of 21 March 1944 the group was alerted to fly on the 22nd. In the night the field order came in. Though many airmen were not aware of much change, the base

PHONEY EXPRESS (Ford-built B-24H-20-FO 42-94833 of the 845th BS, although formerly in the 844th BS/489th BG) is surrounded by other squadron aircraft during a long range mission (*Charles Frudenthal*)

became a beehive of activity that night. Operations (S-3) had to turn the orders into specific directives and briefing notes. Staff bombardiers were busy with problems that come up the next day. Navigators laid out routes and alternatives. The intelligence staff (S-2) began digging into target files for all the data they had on the one chosen for our debut.

Another massed-formation shot of 489th BG Liberators, this time from the 847th BS, over Europe (*Charles Frudenthal*)

They had to estimate the flak facing the flyers and they had to guess what the enemy fighters would do.

'At the same time, Materiel (S-4) had to man-handle the hardware (aircraft, gas, bombs, flak suits, ammunition, parachutes, oxygen, guns, Mae Wests, radio crystals, etc.). They also had to perform the many checks necessary to ensure that the various equipment would be working on the next day. While the airmen slept or tossed (depending on the level of anxiety), the ground machine rolled on . . .'

Woolnough also vividly talks of how a typical mission began;

'At 0315 hours, I was aware that my roommate and I were being a wakened – though I do not remember sleeping. Time to go to the Pre-briefing. I crawled out of the damp bed into the cold, damp room and shuddered into my cold clothes (nothing ever felt crisp and warm in that country . . .'

The target was Berlin – more specifically the Aero Engine factory of the Brandenburgisch Motor Works at Basdorf, 15 miles (24 km) north of the German capital. A fundamental change was taking place. Now, long-range P-51 Mustang fighters were able to go along with the bombers.

Woolnough remembered how it felt during those critical moments when his B-24 Liberator was reaching the target;

'The B-24s ahead seemed to be having no trouble. No fighters and the little bit of flak we had seen so far seemed harmless. We reached the IP at 1325, turned south south-west, and opened out bomb bay doors.

'We could see what looked like a black cap over the spot where the city should be. As we got closer, we could see that the cap was made up of individual bursts of black flak – at our altitude.

'They were using a barrage pattern over the city. Firing at our altitude so we could run into it. The flak really looked harmless. Once in awhile a trace of one would float past my window. Now, we could hear them explode, although it wasn't very loud. Every once in awhile we could hear the pieces rattle off the wings and fuselage as we ran through the debris of a spent round. We almost held our breath during the bomb run.

Following a Liberator mission in early 1944, Maj James Stewart (seated) is joined by fellow Pennsylvanians of the 445th BG for a posed portrait. They are, from left, Keith Dibble, Roger Counselman, Stewart, Joseph Florentino and A Edward Wilen. Stewart commanded a squadron of the 445th BG before moving to group headquarters, and he flew at least 25 combat missions (*Liberator Club*)

B-24 Liberator gunner Hal Erbe leaned into the wind blast to shoot this previously unpublished portrait of a welcome 'little friend' in the form of North American P-51B-NA Mustang 42-106945, coded E9-V, of the 376th FS/361st FG. The group was based at Bottisham, in Cambridgeshire, and had been flying the Mustang since trading in its Thunderbolts in May 1944 (*Hal Erbe*)

In moments, it got worse.'

B-24H 41-29434 *TERRY AND THE PIRATES*, piloted by 1Lt William Terry, was suddenly flying upside down over the target. A crew member on another Liberator 'wondered what the heck he was doing in that attitude'. Another crew member said, 'Suddenly I saw directly ahead and below a bomber with one tail missing. Mid-air collision! It was trying desperately to stay upright, but finally it slid off to the left and slowly turned belly up with its bomb bay open, the bombs still in the racks. Then it went into a helpless spin. The realisation struck me that a bomber could spin in as easily as a single-seater'.

As a result of the mid-air between two Liberators (neither in Woolnough's group), a crewman on another B-24 'saw two props sailing through the air from one plane, and I watched the other minus a tail as it went through a cloud. Our tail gunner got a bird's eye view of everything that happened that day over Berlin. He was so terrified that he had to be helped out of the turret'. *TERRY* and another B-24H were lost, but the 446th BG 'The Flying Deck' dropped 1112 bombs of the 100-lb (45-kg) M-47A1 variety on the target – part of a much larger effort now that American 'heavies' had finally begun pounding the nerve centre of the Third Reich.

The first Eighth Air Force Liberator to complete 50 missions was *BOMERANG*, a B-24D-1-CO (41-23722) of the 328th BS/93rd BG. The name of the aircraft was a mis-spelling, not a pun. In April 1944, the Eighth relieved this veteran and sent it home for a publicity tour. A veteran of the *Tidal Wave* mission against Ploesti, it travelled the USA and visited plants where workers built aircraft and powerplants.

BERLIN AGAIN

There was a big raid flown against Berlin by the Eighth on Easter Sunday 1944, which fell on 9 April. A total of 542 bombers from the 1st, 2nd and 3rd Air Divisions were launched sent to bomb targets in the Berlin area at Rahmen, Marienburg, Tutow, Posen, Rostock and Warnemunde. 402 aircraft reached the targets, although 32 were reported lost or missing. The weather was bad, for there was lots of cloud at the rendezvous point. As viewed by Will Lundy of the 44th BG's 'Eightballs', the mission was a tough one;

'Very unfavourable weather confronted the 44th BG's formation, so a recall was issued. Some of the planes had dropped their bombs prior to receiving the recall, however. Very heavy flak and enemy aircraft attacks were experienced, with the 68th BS had one aircraft that did not return. This was the *PISTOL PACKIN'MAMA* (B-24D-1-CO 42-72858, coded 'U'), piloted by 1Lt Hiram C Palmer.

'The mission report states that the right wing of the plane was damaged, so the pilot headed for Sweden at 18,000 ft (5486 m). All engines apparently were operating under control. It landed at Bulltofta Airfield, in Sweden, with considerable damage to the (*text continues on page 64*)

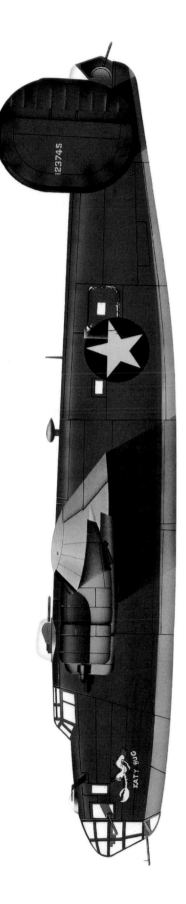

1
B-24D-1-CO 41-23745 *KATY BUG* of the 93rd BG, Alconbury, November 1942

2
B-24D-25-CO 41-24282 *RUTH-LESS* of the 506th BS/44th BG, Shipdham, summer 1943

3

B-24D-25-CO 42-24226 *JOISEY BOUNCE* of the 330th BS/93rd BG, Hardwick, summer 1943

4

B-24D-20-CF 42-63980 *MISSOURI MAULER* of the 567th BS/389th BG, Hethel, summer 1943

5
B-24D-30-CO 42-40128 *WAR BABY/BALL OF FIRE THE III* of the 328th BS/93rd BG, Hardwick, autumn 1943

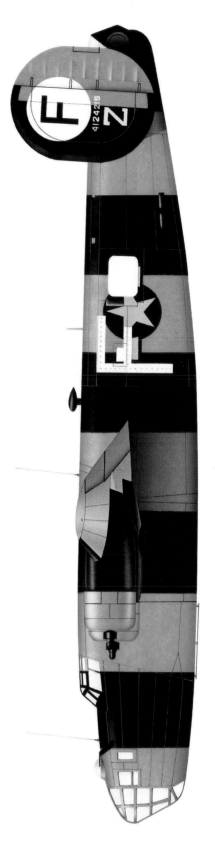

6
B-24D-20-CO 41-24215 *LUCKY GORDON*, assembly ship for the 445th BG, Tibenham, autumn 1943

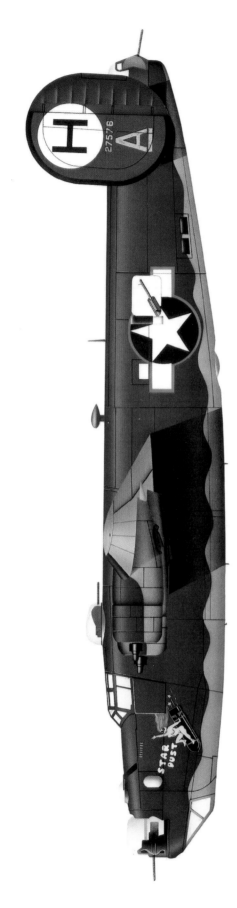

7

B-24H-1-FD 42-7576 *STAR DUST* of the 705th BS/446th BG, Bungay, autumn 1943

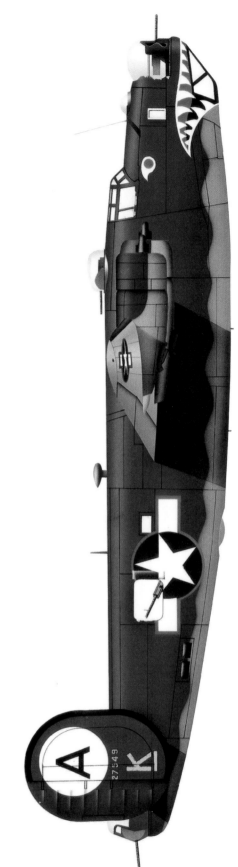

8

B-24H-1-FO 42-7549 of the 67th BS/44th BG, Shipdham, November 1943

9
B-24D-1-CO 41-23689 *MINERVA*, assembly ship for the 392nd BG, Wendling, January 1944

10
B-24D-5-CO 41-23809 *You cawn't miss it!*, assembly ship for the 448th BG, Bungay, February 1944

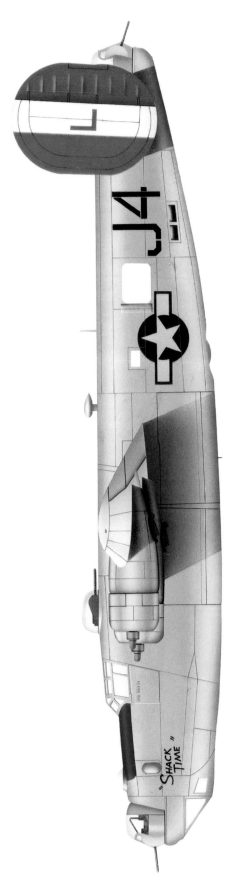

11
B-24J-155-CO 44-40275 *"Shack Time"* of the 753rd BS/458th BG, Horsham St Faith, spring 1944

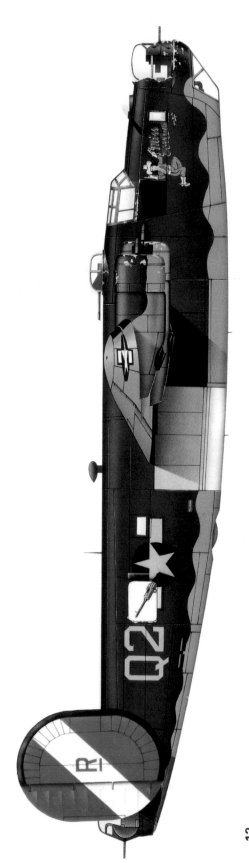

12
B-24H-15-CO 42-52559 *Miss Fortune* of the 790th BS/467th BG, Rackheath, spring 1944

13
B-24H-20-CF 42-95011 of the 856th BS/492nd BG, North Pickenham, May 1944

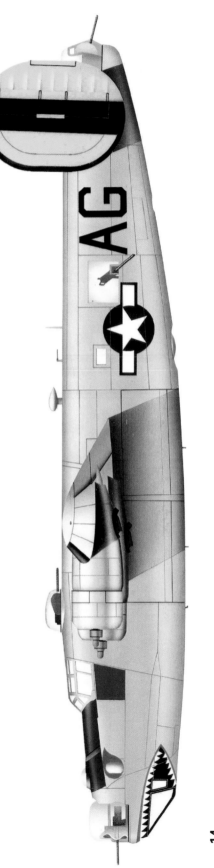

14
B-24J-5-FO 42-50829 of the 330th BS/93rd BG, Hardwick, summer 1944

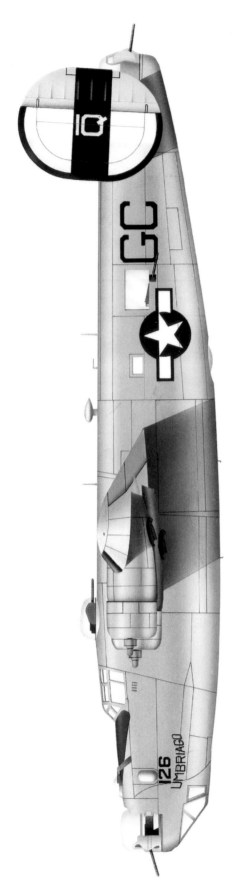

15
B-24H-25-DT 42-51128 *UMBRIAGO* of the 579th BS/392nd BG, Wendling, summer 1944

16
B-24H-15-CF 41-29487 *BLASTED EVENT!* of the 700th BS/445th BG, Tibenham, summer 1944

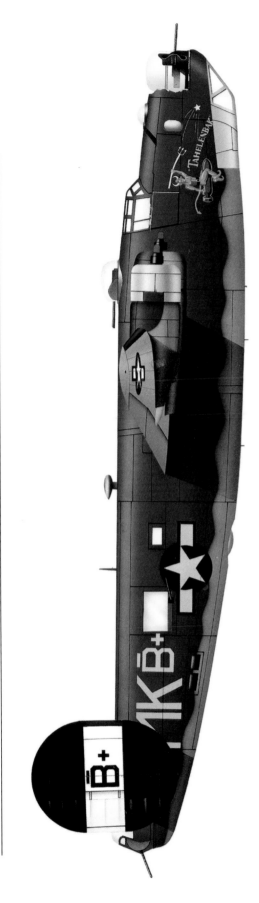

17
B-24H-20-FO 42-94921 *"TAHELENBAK"* of the 701st BS/445th BG, Tibenham, summer 1944

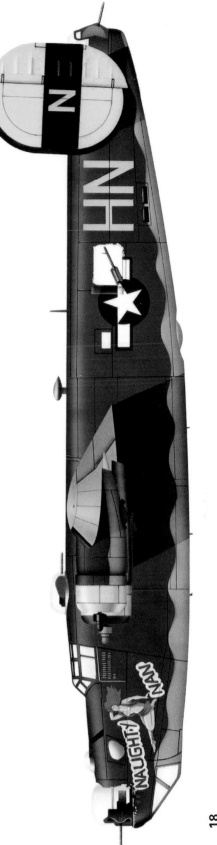

18
B-24H-15-FO 42-52594 *NAUGHTY NAN* of the 705th BS/446th BG, Bungay, summer 1944

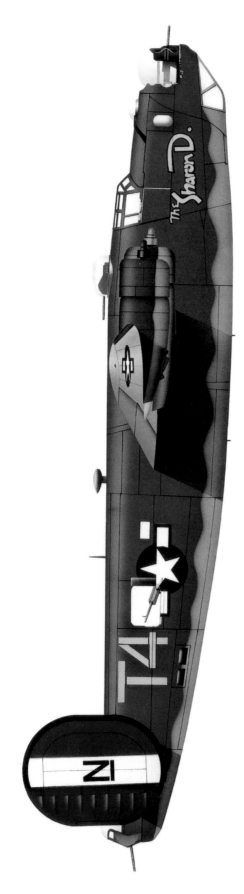

19
B-24H-15-FO 42-94759 *The Sharon D.* of the 489th BG, Halesworth, summer 1944

20
B-24J-145-CO 44-40073 *ARK ANGEL* of the 853rd BS/491st BG, Metfield, summer 1944

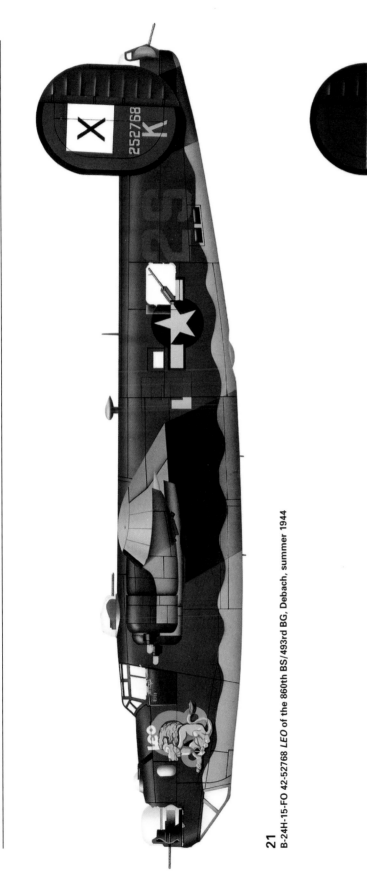

21
B-24H-15-FO 42-52768 *LEO* of the 860th BS/493rd BG, Debach, summer 1944

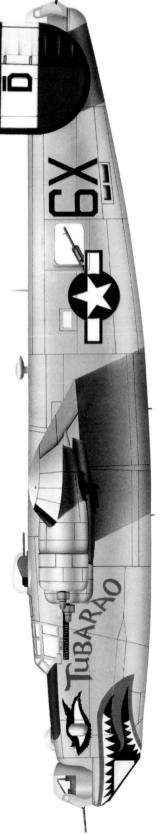

22
B-24J-145-CO 44-40101 *TUBARAO* of the 854th BS/491st BG, North Pickenham, September 1944

23
B-24H-25-FO 42-95049 *Fearless Fosdick/writ by hand* of the 67th BS/44th BG, Shipdham, autumn 1944

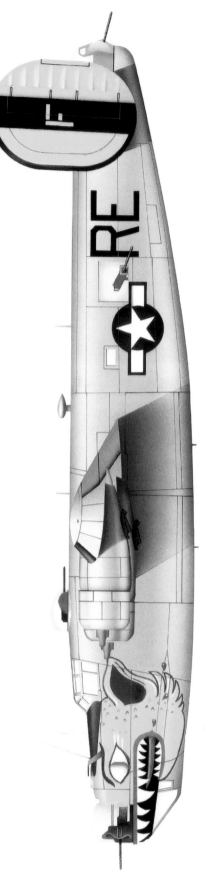

24
B-24J-5-DT 42-51376 of the 329th BS/93rd BG, Hardwick, autumn 1944

25
B-24J-65-CF 44-10599 *WiNDY WiNNiE* of the 712th BS/448th BG, Seething, autumn 1944

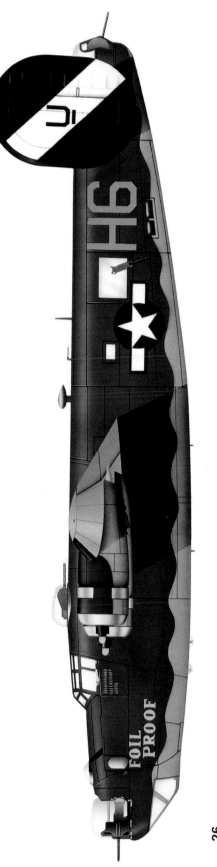

26
B-24H-20-FO 42-94805 *FOIL PROOF* of the 735th BS/453rd BG, Old Buckenham, autumn 1944

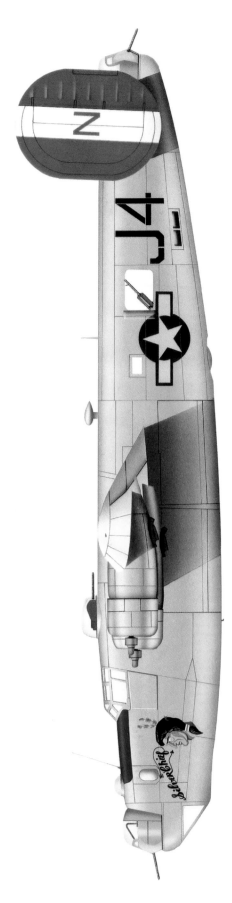

27
B-24J-150-CO 44-40201 *Silver Chief* of the 753rd BS/458th BG, Horsham St Faith, autumn 1944

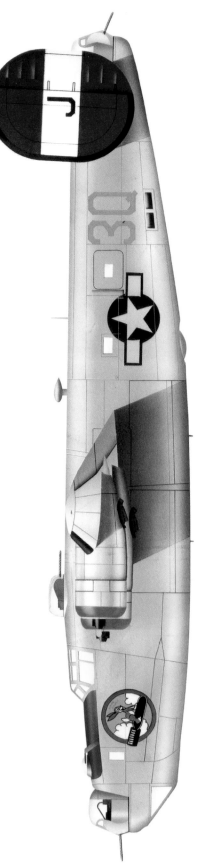

28
B-24J-145-CO 44-40117 *HARE POWER* of the 852nd BS/491st BG, North Pickenham, autumn 1944

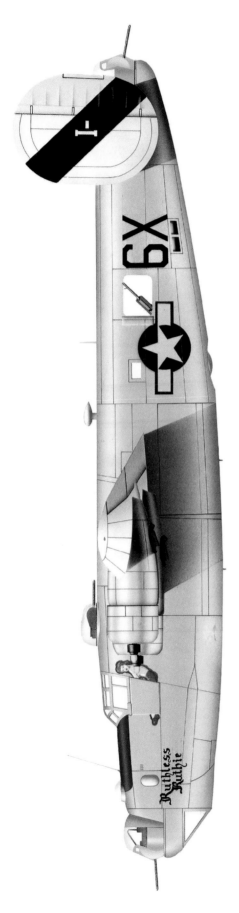

29
B-24J-155-CO 44-40317 *Ruthless Ruthie* of the 854th BS/491st BG, North Pickenham, autumn 1944

30
B-24M-5-FO 44-50527 *HAZEE* of the 732nd BS/453rd BG, Old Buckenham, spring 1945

This Douglas-built B-24H-30-DT Liberator (42-51190) was caught at Mount Farm (Station 234), in Oxfordshire, in the spring of 1944 by the sharply-focused camera of Robert Astrella. The bomber seems to have a fresh, new look, and already wears the rather muted markings of the 18th BS/34th BG at Mendlesham. The front half of the stabiliser has been painted red (note that only the last two digits in its serial remain visible) and the rudder boasts the single balck letter 'H'. The bomber was lost in a mid-air collision on 19 July 1944. There were no survivors (*Robert Astrella*)

right wing and nose section. *PISTOL PACKIN'MAMA* had completed 29 missions, but only half of her 30th, and proudly displayed 29 pistols, not bombs, on her left nose section.'

The aircraft's engineer explained that;

'We were attacked on our way to the target by the yellow-nosed Bf 109s and Fw 190s. About the third or fourth pass, we got hit in our right wing, It missed the No 4 engine, but that big hole in the wing, compounded by the large section of the skin peeled back, caused us to pull 60 inches of mercury on all four of our engines. We also took a hit in the nose area, which disabled our nose wheel landing gear.

'We couldn't keep up with the formation, even with absolute maximum power, so we slowly started dropping back. At the time of the hit, we were near Hamburg, Germany, so we headed for Sweden. Several German fighters started chasing us, but they didn't shoot at us! They could see we were in trouble, and headed for Sweden and out of the war.

'We were over Denmark by this time, close to Malmo, in Sweden. Before any further German fighter attacks could be made, a group of Swedish fighters (probably FFVS J 22s) came up to protect us by chasing off the German planes. Then, they led us to an airfield in Malmo.

'We couldn't get our nose gear down, even though we tried to lower it manually. It was shot up pretty badly. The crew was throwing everything overboard to make it less of a drag on those engines. We couldn't hold out any longer, so we followed the Swedes to Bulltofta, the no-runway airfield, in Malmo. With our main gear down, nose wheel up, we went in for a crash landing on the grass field. I was stationed in the bomb bay, where I could see our pilot, and the rest of the crew was back in the tail section where they could see each other. After the pilots had landed on the main gears and was slowing down, the four (crew) in the tail started moving slowly forward in order to allow the nose to lower slowly, following my hand signals.

'The nose settled down slowly until it started skimming up the grass and dirt. Then it started digging in. Since I was standing in the bomb bay at the edge of the flight deck, I had to lift my feet up to keep the dirt from burying them. That was the most beautiful crash landing I've ever seen or heard about, anytime, any place. We were shaken and very scared, but none of us were injured.'

Eight of the crew eventually returned to duty when the Swedes began repatriating Americans later in 1944.

AND THE 467th

The 467th BG entered combat as part of the 96th CBW/2nd Air Division on 10 April 1944 flying olive-drab Liberators with the letter 'P' enclosed in a white circle. The group's only commander throughout the war was Col Albert J Shower – he was the only CO to bring a combat group to Europe, lead it throughout all of its missions, and take it home after victory was attained. Col Shower was still attending reunions with his men when this narrative was written near the turn of the century.

The 467th BG flew from Rackheath (Station 145), in Norfolk, initially with B-24Hs and later with B-24J/L/Ms. The group completed 212 missions and 5538 sorties, and its squadrons (and codes) were the 788th BS (X7), 789th BS (6A), 790th BS (Q2) and 791st BS (4Z). Later on, the 467th boasted a red fin with a white slash, and an individual aircraft letter inside the slash. This group was known as the 'Rackheath Aggies'.

The 492nd BG joined the Eighth Air Force and launched its first mission on 11 May 1944, flying from North Pickenham (Station 143), in Norfolk. The combat career of this group was to be brief, however, for it was disbanded on 7 August 1944 and then reformed as a special operations unit, known as the 'Carpetbaggers', at Harrington, in Northamptonshire. The 492nd's nomenclature replaced the provisional 801st BG for this second, and separate, duty.

During its three-month tenure with B-24H/Js, the 492nd's only commander was Col Eugene H. Snavely. The group flew a 'mere' 66 missions, and its squadrons (and their codes) were the 856th BS (5Z), 857th BS (9H), 858th BS (9A) and 859th BS (X4).

During its short time as a bomb group, the 492nd gained something of a reputation for being jinxed. Its crews had difficulty adjusting to the procedures for forming up and flying formation, with the resulting errors making them vulnerable to the Luftwaffe. Contrary to myth, German pilots never singled out a specific bomb group for their ministrations, but

93rd BG B-24Ms drop supplies for American paratroopers at Wesel, in Germany, on 24 March 1945. Liberator groups had flown similar missions the previous September in support of the 1st Allied Airborne Army, which had been sent in to seize the bridges at Arnhem, Eindhoven and Nijmegen, in Holland (*via William N Hess*)

On a 1944 mission to Euskirchen, in Germany, bombs from Liberators of the 713th BS/448th BG plummet toward the earth. The smoke trail to the right of the photo was created by a 'Skymarker' bomb, which was the term used by crews for a smoke bomb dropped by the PFF (Pathfinder) aircraft to create a visual cue for the bomb drop by the remainder of the formation. This was a simple, but effective, method intended to permit an entire combat group to put all of its bombs on target, although a study after the war showed that estimates of bombing precision were exaggerated (*via 'King' Schultz*)

without any effort on their part, the 492nd often made itself the 'meat on the table'. The group lost an incredible 57 Liberators in the span of just three months while flying 66 missions and 1606 sorties.

As for the 'Carpetbaggers', their job involved a series of 'hush-hush', unorthodox missions behind enemy lines. There were 'Carpetbagger' outfits around the world, their title having its origins in the period following the American Civil War, when northern politicians and merchants descended on a defeated South to take advantage of a people seeking to rebuild. They arrived carrying luggage made from carpetry. Today, the term means an outsider who intrudes on another's turf – an apt name.

B-24s began 'Carpetbagger' operations from England in 1944, using a new base at Harrington (Station 179), in Northamptonshire. After a brief period as the 801st BG(P), the 'Carpetbaggers' took over the identity of the 492nd BG on 13 August 1944. They initially flew B-24Ds with tail guns only (and later B-24Hs), using as many a 40 aircraft to deliver supplies and agents to resistance forces in occupied territory. They carried out their missions at night, in appalling weather, where flying conditions and terrain were the greatest enemies.

Typically, their aircraft were black, with non-standard glazed noses and exhaust covers to reduce their visual profile at night. They were, of course, part of a larger worldwide special operations effort. Their 'black world' activities meant not only aircraft modifications, but long-range endurance flights and techniques not seen elsewhere. As well as dropping agents and material in the Eighth's area of responsibility, Black Liberators operated across the globe – indeed, one aircraft from the 492nd BG was even spotted as far away as Burma.

The 'Carpetbagger' missions in Europe required the Liberator for its long-range capabilities, and crews praised the aircraft mightily. The need for 'Carpetbagger' operations declined sharply after the autumn of 1944, the 492nd's substantial fleet of B-24s quietly carried out their night work right through to VE-Day.

It should be noted that a handful of Liberators also equipped a special unit that carried out a campaign to disrupt German radio communications on the continent.

ENTER THE 489th

The 489th BG, commanded by Col Ezekial W Napier, began operations from Halesworth (Holton), in Suffolk, in B-24H, and later flew J-models as well. The 489th was destined to complete 106 missions consisting of 2998 sorties, and to produce the only Medal of Honor recipient among Liberator flyers in Europe in the Eighth Air Force's area of responsibility. The group's squadrons (and their codes) were the 844th BS (4R), 845th BS (S4), 846th BS (8R) and 847th BS (T4).

The 489th BG flew its first combat mission on 30 May 1944 to Oldenburg, in Germany, and subsequently bombed targets in northern France in support of the Allied invasion of Normandy. The group's deputy commander was Lt Col Leon R Vance Jr, a 1939 graduate of the US Military Academy at West Point, New York. Although an experienced pilot, and leader, he had no combat time.

Vance participated in the 30 May mission as group air commander, being in charge of the bombing formation. In this role he was not expected necessarily to pilot an aircraft, instead flying in the 489th BG's lead bomber, along with two pilots. Freed of immediate responsibility for the aircraft, Vance could focus on the rest of the group as the mission progressed. The lead aeroplanes were called 'PFF ships', or Pathfinders, and were equipped with H2X radar, also dubbed AN/APS-15 and called *Mickey* by some. The business end of the radar was located in a thimble-shaped dome which protruded from the lower fuselage where a ball turret otherwise would have been.

On 5 June 1944 (the eve of the Allied invasion) Vance flew his second – and last – mission. The target was a German coastal defence complex near Wimereaux and, again, Vance was group air commander. His aircraft was Douglas-built B-24H 41-28690 *MISSOURI BELLE*, piloted by Capt Louis Mazure and 1Lt Earl 'Rocket' Carper (not, as in nearly all published accounts, Casper). The bomber (and crew), except for Vance, belonged to the 66th BS/44th BG, and it was flying the mission because the 489th did not yet have its own *Mickey* aircraft.

Approaching the target, Vance ordered the group to release bombs, but found that his aircraft had a mechanical release fault. He ordered Mazure to make a 360-degree turn and set up a second run-in on the target. The bombardier used

The 22 April 1944 mission to the German city of Hamm by several bomb groups had a horrific aftermath, with Luftwaffe fighters chasing the Liberators all the way back to England as darkness closed in. The airfield controller turned runway lights on, then off, again and again as German fighters weaved amongst the returning B-24s. Bomber crews in reply switched their landing lights on, then off, then on. One officer on the ground at the 448th BG station at Seething blasted away at low-flying German aircraft with an M3A1 carbine! Meanwhile, in darkness and confusion, Liberators – some of them damaged – piled up upon one another, resulting in the three-aircraft mess seen here the following morning at the 448th BG's Norfolk base (*via 'King' Schultz*)

The ability of American industry to produce warplanes far exceeded the Luftwaffe's capacity to shoot them down. In this panorama of the Consolidated factory in San Diego, silvery B-14J-145-CO Liberators stretch almost as far as the eye can see. The future *HARE POWER* of the 852nd BS/491st BG (the subject of colour profile No 28 in this volume) is the fourth aircraft in this line-up, and it already wears its serial 44-40117. The San Diego plant's impressive performance totalled 7500 Liberators, but Ford in Willow Run built them faster, turning out a complete B-24, plus components of two others, every 56 minutes! (*via Allan G Blue*)

manual release to drop, but one 500-lb (227-kg) bomb became 'hung' in the bay.

Simultaneously, 42-94830 became the focal point of a deadly box of flak, and one burst exploded near the wing root and shredded the bomber with slivers of white-hot steel. The impact killed Mazure instantly, whilst Carper suffered serious wounds, along with other crew members. Three of the Liberator's engines halted, and the bomber reared toward the stalling point, with its remaining engine failing.

Vance, who had been standing on the flight platform behind the pilots, recovered from the shock of the blast and lunged forward, burdened by flying gear and the gyrations of the aircraft, to attempt to feather the crippled engines. He could not reach the switches.

He glanced down and discovered that his right foot was severed, and remained attached to his leg only by the tendons, and was jammed inextricably behind the co-pilot's seat and attachments. Unable to stand fully, or exchange places with the injured Carper, Vance stretched as far as he could from his semi-upright position and switched off the three damaged engines and feathered the fourth. Realising that the shattered instruments were also useless, Vance forced a side-window down a few inches to spot the southern coast of England. With help from the radar operator, who had by now fought his way forward, Vance was able to set up the B-24H to ditch but, because of the hung bomb, he ordered the crew to bail out.

Before Vance could seek a way to extract his near-severed foot in order to parachute, a voice on the intercom convinced him that one crew member was too badly injured to jump. Although the Liberator was never the best aircraft in a ditching situation, Vance saw no choice but to attempt to set down on the water. The horrendous impact was punctuated by oxygen bottles exploding, and the next thing Vance knew he was floating on the surface attached to some wreckage.

He then had to fight to keep himself from lapsing into unconsciousness. After an hour immersed in the cold waters of the Channel, Vance was rescued by a British ASR (Air Sea Rescue) boat and, on being hauled abroad, joked, 'Don't forget to bring my foot in'. He was heading home to recover, and trying to find a way to return to combat flying, when he went down on a C-54 Skymaster carrying wounded and crippled veterans over the North Atlantic on 26 July 1944.

Vance was awarded the Medal of Honor, and the air base in his home town of Enid, Oklahoma (today, a pilot-training base) is named in his honour.

ARRIVAL OF THE 486th AND 487th BGs

The 486th and 487th BGs began operations on 7 May 1944. Both were made part of the 92nd Combat Bomb Wing, 3rd Air Division, and both were soon to become all-B-17 outfits, the 3rd Air Division going out of the Liberator business in late 1944 and leaving the 2nd Air Division as the owner of all Liberators in the 'Mighty Eighth'. But although their Liberator days were brief, these groups supported the invasion of Europe and the beginning of a land war on the continent.

The 486th BG, flying from Sudbury (Station 174), and commanded initially by Col Glendon P Overing, was made up of squadrons (and codes) as follows: 832nd BS (3R), 833rd BS (4M), 834th BS (2S) and the 835th BS (H8). The group initially flew B-24H/Js.

The 487th BG at Lavenham (Station 137) included these squadrons (and codes): 836th BS (2G), 837th BS (4F), 838th BS (2C) and the 839th BS (R5). Its first commander was Col Beirne Lay Jr, who had been one of the first Eighth Air Force staff officers, and later became co-author, with Sy Bartlett, of the novel and screenplay *Twelve O'clock. High*.

Lay's interest in writing was well known, for he had been the author of *I Wanted Wings*, a book read by many in his outfit that was made into a 1941 film starring Ray Milland and Veronica Lake. A crew member in a Liberator from his group recalls that, 'We were always a little nervous on a mission, figuring he might be looking for new material'. Lay's best-known work was published in 1948, and later became a film starring Gregory Peck.

During an attack on German marshalling yards at Chateaudun in north-eastern France on an unusually sunny European day (11 May 1944), Lay was shot down 'right in front of me', remembers veteran Bill Colburn. He parachuted to earth, evaded capture, and wrote another book about this experience entitled *I've Had It*.

His 487th BG also began with B-24H/J models, but (like the 486th BG) it was required to convert to the B-17G Flying Fortress from 1

They were called 'The Ringmasters'. They were the 491st BG, and they went to war from North Pickenham (Station 143), in Norfolk. At least 25 Liberators are visible in this panorama of a mission taking shape in 1944 (*via Clyde Gerdes*)

Sitting on the Marston matting that was a familiar sight at many bases, Ford-built B-24J-20-FO Liberator 44-48832 of the 707th BS/446th BG 'Bungay Buckaroos' was away from home base visiting Chalgrove (Station 465), in Oxfordshire, when photographed in late 1944 (*via Norman Taylor*)

August 1944. Other 3rd Air Division Liberator groups made this change soon afterward.

D-DAY LANDINGS

By the time the long-awaited Allied invasion (Operation *Overlord*) of the continent began, rural folk in England were accustomed to quiet mornings being broken by the sound of aircraft overhead and warming up on the ground – and it happened again on the morning of 6 June 1944. This time, many residents around Eighth Air Force bases believed that something special was up. Typical was the situation at Bungay, where the 'Buckaroos' of the 446th BG were caught up in a frenzy of activity.

Briefings were underway for commanders and crews, while maintenance men tested systems and ran up engines. One 446th BG veteran remembers that 2nd Air Division Field Order No 328 was 'probably the longest and most detailed ever teletaped to a B-24 base'. The order directed aircraft from the division's 2nd, 14th, 20th and 96th combat wings provide over 100 aircraft each.

It will remain forever unclear whether Liberators were tasked to bomb German beachline fortifications at Omaha Beach, the bloodiest of the five invasion beaches during Operation *Neptune*, the amphibious part of the *Overlord* invasion. There, almost everything went wrong. The Eighth Air Force despatched 1198 heavy bombers to attack the areas around the beaches and made an unsuccessful attempt to launch 528 more – cloud cover prevented all but 37 of the latter aircraft from getting aloft. It appears that Fortresses, not Liberators, were assigned to Omaha, but no bombers appeared when expected.

As members of the 446th noted, orders prohibited short-run bombing because of the ground troops waiting offshore during the preliminary air attack. 'Heavies' were directed to fly over their targets in six-ship flights. A H2X pathfinder accompanied every third flight in case weather prevented visual bombing. Their orders were clear and detailed. No second runs. No second chances. No aborted flights after leaving England. Any aircraft returning through the Channel would be fired upon.

The first heavy bombers took off as early as 0200, but those which followed were seriously delayed by the tricky weather. Although 2nd Air Division B-24s were technically led by the 446th BG's *RED ASS* (B-24H-25-FO 42-95203 of the group's 706th BS, flown by Col Jacob Brogger), the first bombs to be dropped were actually delivered by 44th BG aircraft a full three minutes before any other group thanks to a helpful tailwind!

French villages on the roads leading to and from the beachhead were targeted for bombing. Leaflets had been dropped in the days prior to the raid to alert civilians to the dangers of living in an area about to be bombed. In spite of having clear maps and locations, the 3rd Air Division crews approaching these targets were unable to see through cloud cover during their raids as the morning of the invasion unfolded. Fewer than 40 per cent of the 3rd's Liberators dropped as scheduled.

By early afternoon, 73 of the 2nd Air Division's Liberators were bombing targets near Caen, on the Normandy coast. A sole B-24 from the 487th BG was the only Eighth casualty to enemy fire (the 493rd lost two in a mid-air collision), the Luftwaffe making little effort to get through to the bomber crews as they struggled with weather and navigation frustrations.

The relative calm did not last. At dusk on 'D-Day +1', recalls one Liberator veteran, 'all hell broke loose'. A small number of twin-engined Ju 88 and Me 410 fighters followed Liberators home from the continent. In moments, they had shot down four Liberators of the 34th BG in the airfield pattern at Mendlesham, and two more Liberators were wrecked in a runway collision at Feltwell while taking refuge from Me 410s.

The day after the invasion the weather worsened, and Liberator groups paid a price for supporting the Allied foothold on Europe. At Metfield, the 491st BG was launching a mission when B-24H-35-CF 42-40169 *LUCKY PENNY* rose into the sky. The Liberator's No 4 engine suffered a power failure at a critical moment, and the bomber dropped to earth. Two 1000-lb (454-kg) bombs fell from *LUCKY PENNY* and exploded, killing the crew, damaging half a dozen Liberators parked nearby and shutting down the station.

Better luck shined on navigator 1Lt Ben Isgrig of the 448th BG on 12 June 1944. Near Rennes, his Liberator was swarmed-over by Bf 109s and riddled by gunfire. Isgrig bailed out with his crew, and as he floated down, a Bf 109 turned on him in what looked for certain like a firing pass. Just when Isgrig was sure he was dead, a 352nd FG P-51 Mustang appeared and blew the German out of the sky. Maj George Preddy, the highest-scoring ace in the European theatre, had just saved Isgrig's hide.

LIBERATOR SHIFT

In the summer of 1944, those 3rd Air Division units flying B-24s made the transition to B-17s. The goal was to simplify mission planning by having to deal with only one type of heavy bomber within each air division – the 1st and 3rd with B-17s, and the 2nd with B-24s. The groups that made the heavy bomber switch were the 34th, 486th, 487th, 490th and 493rd BGs. The 'brass' transferred some of the displaced bombers to the Mediterranean to join the Fifteenth Air Force, whilst others went to B-24 units in the 2nd Air Division. For example, a 487th BG bomber named *CHIEF WAPELLO* (B-24H-15-FO 42-52618) went to the 44th BG.

In a related move, the 2nd Air Division gave Liberator groups the option of dispensing with ball turrets – and most did.

Consolidated-built B-24J-155-CO Liberator 44-40317 (coded 6X-I), dubbed *Ruthless Ruthie*, was assigned to the 854th BS/491st BG. It is seen at North Pickenham in September 1944, the bomber having ground-looped off the side of the runway after returning from a mission over Germany with battle damage (*via Norman Taylor*)

Anonymous natural-metal B-24 Liberators follow in line astern on their way to a target in northern Europe (*via Robert F Dorr*)

Liberator men had taken a perverse pride in flying a bomber dubbed 'the box the B-17 came in', and many resented being forced to change from Liberator to Fortress – at first. A 487th BG pilot later said that he became satisfied with the Boeing bomber because it was easier to handle.

Other 3rd Air Division units quickly became the object of the Eighth Air Force leadership's prejudice towards the Flying Fortress. For eaxample, the 34th BG at Mendelsham (Station 156), in Suffolk, commanded by Col Ernest J Wackwitz Jr, only flew B-24H/Js in combat between 23 May and 24 August 1944. By mid-September, all four of its squadrons – 4th BS (Q6), 7th BS (R2), 18th BS (8I) and the 391st BS (3L) – had converted to B-17Gs.

The similarly-fated 490th BG, flying from Eye (Station 134), also in Suffolk, and led by Col Lloyd H Watnee, went into action with B-24H/Js on 7 April and then a stood down on 6 August 1944 in anticipation of receiving B-17Gs. Squadrons (and codes) for the Eye bombers were the 848th BS (7W), 849th BS (W8), 850th BS (7Q) and the 851st BS (S3).

In like manner, the 493rd BG 'Helton's Hellcats' went into action in April 1944 led by Col Elbert 'Butch' Helton, who had previously fought in the Pacific. This group operated from Debach (Station 152), again in Suffolk, and was comprised of these squadrons (and codes): 860th BS (NG), 861st BS (Q4) 862nd BS (8M) and the 863rd BS (O6). All of these bomb groups converted from their practical, olive-drab Liberators (primarily H-models) to elegant and shiny Flying Fortresses during August and September 1944, reflecting the desire of commanders to focus on the Boeing bomber, and leave a sole air division (the 2nd) with B-24s.

491st COMBAT DEBUT

Known as 'The Ringmasters', the 491st BG began flying missions on 2 June 1944 from Metfield (Station 366), in Suffolk, and later (following the disbanding of the 492nd BG) from North Pickenham (Station 143), in Norfolk. The group reported to the 14th CBW and 2nd Air Division.

The 491st BG flew a mixed force of olive-drab and natural-metal Liberators, which were initially marked with a green stabiliser broken by a white bar, and later by a black slash. With Lt Col Carl T Goldenberg as its first commander, 'The Ringmasters' boasted these squadrons – the 852nd BS (coded 3Q), 853rd BS (T8), 854th BS (6X) and 855th BS (VZ). The 491st BG had flown 187 missions by 25 April 1945, racking up 5005 sorties.

Ford-built B-24H-20-FO Liberator 42-95203 of the 706th BS/446th BG wore the snappy appellation *RED ASS* on its slab-sided nose. It was photographed whilst on a mission from Bungay in 1944. The 446th BG 'Bungay Buckaroos' lost 86 Liberators in combat. Although this figure may sound formidable, it is appreciably lower than the losses incurred by the companion 445th and 448th BGs (*via Robert F Dorr*)

As Allied armies advanced across Europe, Liberators were drafted to haul fuel to the troops – especially to Lt Gen George S Patton's armoured Third Army, which had moved so fast that it almost outpaced its supply 'tail'. With crews of just five men each, Liberators with special internal tanks carrying an extra 2000 US gallons of fuel flew 12 'Trucking' missions, adding up to nearly 2000 sorties between 19 and 30 September 1944. The bombers used were from the 44th, 458th, 466th, 467th and 492nd BGs.

That month, during Operation *Market-Garden* (the Allied airborne assault in the Netherlands), hundreds of Liberators were used to airdrop supplies. At Arnhem, Nijmegen and Eindhoven, where British and American paratroopers had ventured 'A Bridge Too Far', low-level parachute drops kept the troops supplied, as they battled inside their precarious bridgehead.

As 1944 drew toward its conclusion, the continent was again draped in the foul, brooding weather that made long-range bombing missions all but impossible. In mid-December, the beleaguered German Army launched a dramatic counter-offensive in the Ardennes, and Allied soldiers began the 'Battle of the Bulge' – a terrible campaign in mid-winter that inflicted high casualties, and unquestionably prolonged the war. Fortresses and Liberators were launched against ground targets for several days of risky tactical bombing, but after 20 December the weather grew so bad they had to stand down for 72 hours.

Some 423 'heavies' were able to get aloft for strikes on German forces in the 'Bulge' on 23 December 1944, but their efforts were largely ineffectual due to the persistent cloud cover. Things improved the next day, when no fewer than 2046 bombers of all types were sent aloft and 1884 reached targets. This effort included 643 Liberators, two of which were lost, while more than 150 were damaged. Additional missions followed on Christmas Day and the day thereafter.

On 27 December, 641 bombers were launched and 575 reached targets. Next day, in better weather, 1275 'heavies' set forth and 1158 dropped bombs on German army and supply targets. The battle on the ground had prevented the Eighth from flying long-range strikes on strategic targets, but a mission was flown deep into Germany for the first time since the middle of the month on 31 December. By now, the outcome of the war was apparent to most, yet on the continent, Allied soldiers were fighting for their lives.

1945

On the European continent, a cruel winter was at work as the world began what would become the most destructive year in human history. By mid-January, the Allies were beginning to contain the German thrust in the 'Bulge', but they had little air power to help them because of the weather.

Some idea of the frigid conditions can be gleaned from notes of the New Year's Day effort aimed at Koblenz, as jotted down by the 458th BG's George A Reynolds;

'A rough one. The target was a bridge over the Moselle at Guls-Koblenz. 27 aircraft dispatched. Very heavy cloud coverage all the way. Ran into headwinds, calculated at 180 mph (290 km/h) from 40 degrees which reduced our ground speed to 20 mph (32 km/h). The mission had to be abandoned 40 miles (64 km) from the IP. Three of our aircraft bombed with other groups. Three ships landed on the continent, short of gas.'

By now, at least, a Liberator could land in France if it couldn't get home, but there, the frigid weather went hand-in-glove with primitive airfields and inadequate repair facilities.

Despite the moisture and murk, the Eighth Air Force's heavy bomber force pressed on. Amid horrendous snow, ice and sub-zero temperatures, the 2nd Air Division sent eight bomb groups against German targets on

By 1945 an 'aluminum overcast' of natural-metal warplanes was filling the skies of Europe, but many olive-drab Liberators were still on the scene. 'We simply never got around to removing the paint', said 489th BG group bombardier Capt Charles Frudenthal when quizzed about the OD B-24s that were still in service in 1945. A perfect example is this bomber (Ford-built B-24J-FO 42-94800, coded 4R-D), flown by 1Lt John F 'Jack' McMullen of the 489th BG, which wore a four-leafed clover on its starboard side (not visible here), but had no popular nickname (*Charles Frudenthal*)

Ford-built B-24H-20-FO Liberator 42-94852, coded T4-**K**, of the 845th BS/489th BG is seen at Mount Farm (Station 234) in mid-1944 (*Robert Astrella*)

This Consolidated-built B-24J Liberator, coded H6-W underline and nicknamed *Linda Lou*, served with the 735th BS/453rd BG. It is seen here following an emergency landing in early 1945 at a wintry airfield in liberated Belgium. *Linda Lou* appears to have lost her No 2 engine, and is receiving attention from stepladder and scaffolding in a location that appears both foreboding and very, very cold (*1Lt James Kunklo*)

5 January. Two B-24s of the 491st BG 'The Ringmasters' at North Pickenham, unable to get aloft amid the icing and deteriorating visibility, crashed before the raid was even under way.

Nine days later 360 Flying Fortresses and an identical number of Liberators went after petroleum facilities at Brunswick, Heide, Magdeburg and Stendal. In January and February, the 'heavies' joined Operation *Clarion*, a sustained effort against Germany's rail system. Other targets included submarine pens and shipping yards at Kiel, Hamburg and Bremen.

FEBRUARY WAR

On the third anniversary of the formation of the Eighth Air Force, 3 February 1945, 29 Liberators of the 448th BG travelled to Magdeburg, where they used H2X radar to drop their bombs through 100 per cent cloud cover.

Also in February 1945, the Allied Bomber Offensive shifted much of its attention to knocking out communications and transportation targets in Germany – the RAF by night and the AAF by day, with four-engined 'heavies' of the Eighth and Fifteenth Air Forces converging on the Reich. On 22 February 1945, the Eighth sent forth 4428 'heavies', of which 1372 were able to bomb. Four of the seven bombers that fell in battle were Liberators.

This effort, designated Operation *Clarion*, persisted for a second day

when 1274 bombers launched, 1211 bombed and five Liberators were lost – one in combat and four due to collisions or ditchings.

Ray F Sounders Jr was a flight engineer/gunner (top turret) with the 703rd BS/445th BG, and here he remembers a 9 March mission to Munster;

'As we left the English Channel, on the way we lost the No 4 engine and could not keep up with our group (the 445th), so we eventually ended up flying with the 458th BG. On this mission we had a photographer with us, and he captured a picture of a B-24 which was on our right, hit by ack-ack We were flying *HITLER'S HEARSE* (an aircraft whose serial has not surfaced in the years since the war) on this mission and came back with the No 4 propeller feathered.'

Sounder's recollection sounds so prosaic that it is easy to forget a war was still on. To be sure, the fighting had gotten easier in some respects. Liberator crews finished their tours of duty (at first 25 missions, then 30 and finally 35) and went home to be replaced by fresh crews. But Luftwaffe pilots could not be relieved or refreshed, and the air campaign was wearing them down. Although the Allied Bomber Offensive still had not destroyed the Luftwaffe, or the German aircraft industry – although it had

This Consolidated-built B-24J-5-FO Liberator (42-50773) of the 707th BS/446th BG has its bomb bay doors open while the bombardier makes final calculations during a raid on German marshalling yards at Aschaffenburg on 25 February 1945. In the final weeks of the war, natural metal finish was the order of the day for Eighth Air Force Liberators (*via* Warren M Bodie)

Upon reaching England, pilot 1Lt Edward 'King' Schultz of the 713th BS/448th BG learned that newly-arriving Liberators were sent first to depots like Burtonwood to be field-modified for combat. This process included adding armour plate, like the olive-drab 'slab' seen here beneath the co-pilot's window on Schultz's otherwise natural-metal B-24H-15-FO (42-95185), nicknamed 'DO BUNNY', the first word being pronounced 'doe'. Schultz, kneeling, poses with other crew members and, their ubiquitous bicycles, which littered bomber ramps across East Anglia (*via* 'King' Schultz)

The aircraft closest to the camera here is Ford-built B-24M-10-FO Liberator 44-50748, coded topline J-GJ, of the 506th BS/44th BG and nicknamed *BIG HEADED KID*. The original copy of this image is dated 24 April 1945, which was the day before Liberator groups halted their offensive operations in Europe (*via Will Lundy*)

The crucially important Consair A6 tail turret on the B-24. Designed and constructed by the manufacturer, this example features staggered guns with short barrels, denoting that it was fitted to an early-build Liberator (*via Norman Taylor*)

B-24H-15-FO 42-95260, coded WQ-B (farthest from the camera), was nicknamed *LILI MARLENE* by its pilot, Lt Perritie. Belonging to the 68th BS/44th BG, the aircraft survived in combat from May through to 28 December 1944, when it crashed at Shipham after aborting its mission due to engine trouble. The bomber's pilot, Lt Jesse Bledsoe, and his entire crew were killed (*via Will Lundy*)

This Ford-built B-24J-5-FO (42-50806), coded WQ-E, of the 68th BS/44th BG is seen following its return to the USA in mid-1945 (*via Will Lundy*)

inflicted serious damage on both - the Reich was running out of pilots.

On 14 March, no fewer than 2000 Eighth Air Force aircraft were aloft pounding industrial and communications facilities in western Germany. A week later, heavy bombers attacked 11 airfields which Messerschmitt Me 262 jets were known to be operating out of. On 24 March 1945, Allied troops secured a bridgehead at Remagen and crossed the Rhine. That day, 237 Liberators airdropped supplies to airborne forces across the Rhine, sustaining 14 losses.

The crossing of the Rhine was unquestionably the last straw for the battered Reich. In late March, the US First Army captured Cologne. Reportedly, a downed B-24 crew member was with them when they liberated a supply of a fragrance long denied to the world – the famous *4711 Eau de Cologne*, made by *Parfumeria Fabrick Glockengasse*, and named for the address of the factory – itself untouched by Allied bombs!

This B-24J Liberator of the 564th BS/389th BG was seen seconds away from landing at Bradley Field, Connecticut, soon after returning from Europe in May 1945 (*Mike Moffitt*)

This unmarked, and factory-fresh, B-24M-FO Liberator was also photographed at Bradley Field, Connecticut, in July 1945, parked amongst other 44th FG combat veterans (*Mike Moffitt*)

JET FIGHTERS

The German jet fighters made bomber crews edgy (see *Osprey Aircraft of the Aces 17 - German Jet Aces* for further details). On 4 April, Col Troy Crawford, commander of the 446th BG, was riding in a de Havilland Mosquito shepherding the 'Bungay Buckaroos' in a raid on the jet fighter base at Dortmund. The 'Mossie' swung down from higher altitude to look over the bomber formation, and a Liberator crew mistook the twin-engined aircraft for a twin-jet Me 262. Gunners blasted away and sent the Mosquito careening through the bomber swarm, now fired upon by gunners from other B-24s.

Crawford bailed out, was briefly held captive by the Germans, and

The first Eighth Air Force Liberator to complete 50 combat missions was B-24D-1-CO 41-23722 *BOMERANG* of the 328th BS/93rd BG. It returned to the United States in April 1944 for a War Bond tour, and is seen here looking decidedly worse for wear after criss-crossing the USA. Note that it is still wearing a subdued national insignia (minus the 'bars'), with the white darkened to a dull gray – a characteristic of all bombers supplied to the Eighth early on. One of *BOMERANG's* first duties upon returning home was to visit the Pratt & Whitney plant in East Hartford, Connecticut, for the benefit of the employees who assembled engines for the Liberator (*Kent Jaquith*)

1Lt John E 'Jack' Stevens went to war with the 791st BS/467th BG in a bomber named after him. The strident mule adorning *JACK THE RIPPER 'II'* was the mascot of Stevens' alma mater, Colby College, in Maine. *JACK THE RIPPER 'II'* was olive-drab, Ford-built, B-24H-15-FO Liberator 42-52424, and it replaced an earlier bomber also flown by Stevens' crew, which had accumulated considerable battle experience in a short time (*Cindy Stevens*)

negotiated a deal that allowed him and 40 other prisoners to 'run for it' in the direction of the approaching Allied armies. By the time the Liberators of the 'Mighty Eighth' flew their last combat missions over Europe on 25 April, the 'Buckaroos'' commander was safely back at his home station of Bungay.

By April, the defence of the Third Reich by the Luftwaffe had finally come to an end. More than 1300 Liberators and Fortresses were in the air on 7 April when the German fighter force emitted its last gasp, sending up 250 fighters to intercept. They shot down 18 bombers, including two claimed by Me 262s, and two lost to suicide ramming attacks, but it was too little, too late.

Still with plenty of aircraft, but with most of its pilots depleted, the Luftwaffe never again mounted a meaningful effort. A few more interceptions were attempted, but the jets flew their last sorties on 19 April. Six days later Liberators, and other warplanes of the victorious 'Mighty Eighth', flew their final sorties over a Germany that had been largely reduced to rubble.

Adolf Hitler committed suicide in a bunker, Soviet tanks rolled into Berlin and hostilities came to an end in Europe on 7 May 1945. The Eighth Air Force promptly mounted a campaign to show ground

Four members of the crew of *JACK THE RIPPER 'II'*. They are, from left to right: T/Sgt Walter Bohnenstiehl, radio operator; S/Sgt Herbert Vaughn, top turret gunner; T/Sgt Louis Marcarelli (to whom this volume is dedicated), flight engineer; and S/Sgt Benjamin Bertalot, tail turret gunner. This crew gathered considerable experience with the Eighth Air Force and then, in a most unusual move, transferred to the Fifteenth Air Force, which had issued a call for seasoned flyers. On a mission with a different crew, Marcarelli was killed on 22 July 1944 (*Cindy Stevens*)

A most unusual sight – a transplanted Eighth Air Force crew serving with the Fifteenth Air Force in Italy. The crew, headed by 1Lt John 'Jack' Stevens (first row, second from right) earned battle honours with the 791st BS/467th BG before being 'tapped' for an unusual move. The idea was to gather a cadre of experienced bomber crews in the Italian theatre, but only a handful of crews made this change. *Silver Queen* was the bomber they acquired at their new home, Caesar Fortunato air base at Lecce, in Italy after joining the 344th BS/98th BG. T/Sgt Louis Marcarelli, is in the second row, third from left (*Cindy Stevens*)

BALL OF FIRE was the nickname assigned to at least seven Liberators in the Eighth Air Force, including two in the 93rd BG – one of which was this brightly-striped form-up ship, adorned in bands of red, yellow and white. Flying over England in this previously unpublished portrait, this Liberator is not the ship with BALL OF FIRE THE III inscribed on its left side which appears as profile No 5 in this volume (Kent Jaquith)

The well-dressed pilot of an Eighth Air Force Liberator never went into action without helmet, goggles, Mae West, leather jacket and oxygen mask. 1Lt Bob Cline, a B-24H pilot of the 489th BG, seems to be posing in the attire for the folks back home. Under a microscope, stencilling on his lifejacket indicates that in accordance with technical orders, it was inspected for safety on 4 April 1944 (Jim Kiernan)

WITCHCRAFT was Ford-built B-24H-15-FO Liberator 42-52534, assigned to the 790th BS/467th BG and occasionally flown by group commander Col Albert J Shower (Vince Re)

In this view of *WITCHCRAFT*, she is seen dropping eight 1000-lb bombs on Berlin, with the bombs from a second Liberator visible between the two clusters of four bombs each. Although smoke pours from the number two engine, this veteran completed 70 missions without suffering a mechanical failure (*Vince Re*)

personnel the contribution they had made to wrecking the Reich – Flying Fortresses and Liberators carried 10,000 men on 'trolley runs' for an extensive sightseeing tour of the ruins of marshalling yards, aircraft plants and cities.

'Many of us never imagined there could be such destruction', said S/Sgt John Foster of the 93rd BG, who had flown missions in both the Eighth and Fifteenth Air Forces. 'All the time we thought they were beating the hell out of us, we were putting them out of business'.

With an H2X *Mickey* radar protruding like a thimble from its lower rear fuselage, this Liberator of the 93rd BG (the much-embattled 'Ted's Traveling Circus') approaches the drop point, when it will send four 1000-lb (454-kg) bombs toward the target (*Gene Hoffman*)

There were two bombers named *TOMMY THUMPER* in the 4th BS/34th BG, and both were flown by 1Lt Warren Thrun. This is believed to be the first of the two ships, which was damaged on 9 May 1944 when flown by another crew. The 34th BG was one of the 3rd Air Division units which was required to convert to the B-17G Flying Fortress (*Richard C Cooney*)

All three photographs on this page show aircraft from the 467th BG in 1945. The top shot features a mix of natural metal and OD Liberators from the 791st BS at Rackheath, whilst the middle and lower views show aircraft from the 789th BS on a supply dropping mission over western Europe near war's end (*all Vince Re*)

Top
Almost the end. More B-24s from the 467th BG (this time from the 790th BS) drop bombs on Traunstein on 25 April 1945 during the very last mission flown by this bomb group on the last day of normal Liberator operations over the Continent. This was mission 212 for 'The Rackheath Aggies' (*Vince Re*)

Above
The end. Consolidated-built B-24M-16-FO 44-50867 of the Second Air Division's 389th BG managed to survive the war in Europe and was returned to the United States, where it was slated for transfer to the Pacific when the war ended. Like so many B-24s, and other legendary warplanes, this one ended up at the storage facility in Kingman, Arizona. And like so many, it was scrapped (*William T Larkins*)

The aftermath. It is 1946, in Enid, Oklahoma. Sharon Drury Vance (later, Keirnan) is four years old. Flanked by her mother, and the commander at the airfield named for her father, the youthful 'Sharon D' wears the Medal of Honor awarded to Lt Col Leon R 'Bob' Vance, the only B-24 Liberator crew member in the Eighth Air Force to receive the highest American award for valour. Today, the medal (which differs in considerable detail to examples of the Medal of Honor awarded in the postwar air force) occupies a spot among memorabilia at the home of Sharon Keirnan in San Diego, California (*AAF*)

VE-DAY TALLY

By the time the surrender was signed, the Liberator had equipped 19 heavy bomb groups in England. When combined with the 15 groups that flew in the Mediterranean, the total of 34 was seven more groups than went into European combat with B-17 Flying Fortresses. In all, B-24 bombers dropped some 452,308 tons of bombs during 226,773 sorties.

A sad postscript ends the tale. Not including airframes classified as 'war weary', in August 1945 the AAF inventory listed 4236 Liberator bombers. By December 1945, the total had fallen to 1103. A year later, in December 1946, the B-24 inventory in the AAF was five aircraft! And in September 1947 – the month an independent United States Air Force came into being, led by the 'bomber generals' who had won the war – the number of Consolidated B-24 Liberator bombers in the American inventory was zero.

The Liberator had done its job.

B-24 UNITS OF THE EIGHTH AIR FORCE

United States Strategic Air Forces in Europe (USSTAF)

Bushey Park (from 15 February 1944)
(responsible for Eighth and Fifteenth Air Forces)

EIGHTH AIR FORCE

Bushey Park (*Widewing*) (to 15 February 1944)
High Wycombe (after 15 February 1944)

VIII Bomber Command (to 15 February 1944)

1st AIR DIVISION

Equipped with B-17s, except one squadron of 482nd BG (814th BS/SI) with a handful of B-24s

2nd AIR DIVISION

2nd Combat Bomb Wing

389th BG 'The Sky Scorpions'
Base – Hethel, from 11/6/43 to 30/5/45
Aircraft – B-24D/H/J/L and M

564th BS (YO)
565th BS (EE)
566th BS (RR)
567th BS (HP)

445th BG
Base – Tibenham, from 4/11/43 to 28/5/45
Aircraft – B-24H/J/L and M

700th BS (RN)
701st BS (MK)
702nd BS (WV)
703rd BS (IS)

453rd BG
Base – Old Buckenham, from 22/12/43 to 9/5/45
Aircraft – B-24H/J/L and M

732nd BS (E3)
733rd BS (F8)
734th BS (E8)
735th BS (H6)

14th COMBAT BOMB WING

44th BG 'Flying Eight Balls'
Base – Cheddington (11/9/42 to 9/10/42)
and Shipdham (10/10/45)
Aircraft – B-24D/H/J/L and M

66th BS (QK)
67th BS (NB)
68th BS (WQ)
506th BS (GJ)

392nd BG 'Crusaders'
Base – Wendling, from 1/8/43 to 15/6/45
Aircraft – B-24H/J/L and M

576th BS (CI)
577th BS (DC)
578th BS (EG)
579th BS (GC)

491st BG 'The Ringmasters'
Base –- Metfield (25/4/44 to 15/8/44) and
North Pickenham (15/8/44 to 4/7/45)
Aircraft – B-24J/L and M

852nd BS (3Q)
853rd BS (T8)
854th BS (6X)
855th BS (VZ)

492nd BG (first organisation)
Base –- North Pickenham, from 14/4/44 to 12/8/44
Aircraft – B-24H and J

856th BS (5Z)
857th BS (9H)
858th BS (9A)
859th BS (X4)

20th COMBAT BOMB WING

93rd BG 'Ted's Traveling Circus'
Base – Alconbury (6/9/42 to 6/12/42) and
Hardwick (6/12/42 to 12/6/45)
Aircraft – B-24D/H/J/L and M

328th BS (GO)
329th BS (RE)
330th BS (AG)
409th BS (YM)

446th BG 'Bungay Buckaroos'
Base – Bungay, from 4/11/43 to 5/7/45
Aircraft – B-24H/J/L and M

704th BS (FL)
705th BS (HN)
706th BS (RT)
707th BS (JU)

448th BG
Base – Seething, from 30/11/43 to 6/7/45
Aircraft – B-24H/J/L and M

712th BS (CT)
713th BS (IG)
714th BS (EI)
715th BS (IO)

489th BG
Base – Halesworth, from 1/5/44 to 29/11/44
Aircraft – B-24H

844th BS (4R)
845th BS (S4)
846th BS (8R)
847th BS (T4)

96th COMBAT BOMB WING

458th BG
Base – Horsham St Faith, from 29/1/44 to 3/7/45
Aircraft – B-24H/J/L and M

752nd BS (7V)

753rd BS (J4)
754th BS (Z5)
755th BS (J3)

466th BG 'The Flying Deck'
Base – Attlebridge, from 7/3/44 to 6/7/45
Aircraft – B-24H/J/L and M

784th BS (T9)
785th BS (2U)
786th BS (U8)
787th BS (6L)

467th BG 'Rackheath Aggies'
Base – Rackheath, from 12/3/44 to 5/7/45
Aircraft – B-24H/J/L and M

788th BS (X7)
789th BS (6A)
790th BS (Q2)
791st BS (4Z)

3rd AIR DIVISION

Equipped primarily with B-17s, plus the following combat groups which commenced conversion to the Flying Fortress in August-September 1944

34th BG
Base – Mendelsham, from 18/4/44 to 7/45
Aircraft – B-24H/J and B-17G

4th BS (Q6)
7th BS (R2)
18th BS (8I)
391st BS (3L)

486th BG
Base – Sudbury, from 3/44 to 25/8/45
Aircraft – B-24H/J and B-17G

832nd BS (3R)
833rd BS (4M)
834th BS (2S)
835th BS (H8)

487th BG
Base – Lavenham, from 4/4/44 to 24/8/45
Aircraft – B-24H/J and B-17G

836th BS (2G)
837th BS (4F)
838th BS (2C)
839th BS (R5)

490th BG
Base – Eye, from 26/4/44 to 24/8/45
Aircraft – B-24H/J and B-17G

848th BS (7W)
849th BS (W8)
850th BS (7Q)
851st BS (S3)

493rd BG 'Helton's Hellcats'
Base – Debach, from 5/44 to 6/8/45
Aircraft – B-24H/J and B-17G

860th BS (NG)
861st BS (Q4)
862nd BS (8M)
863rd BS (O6)

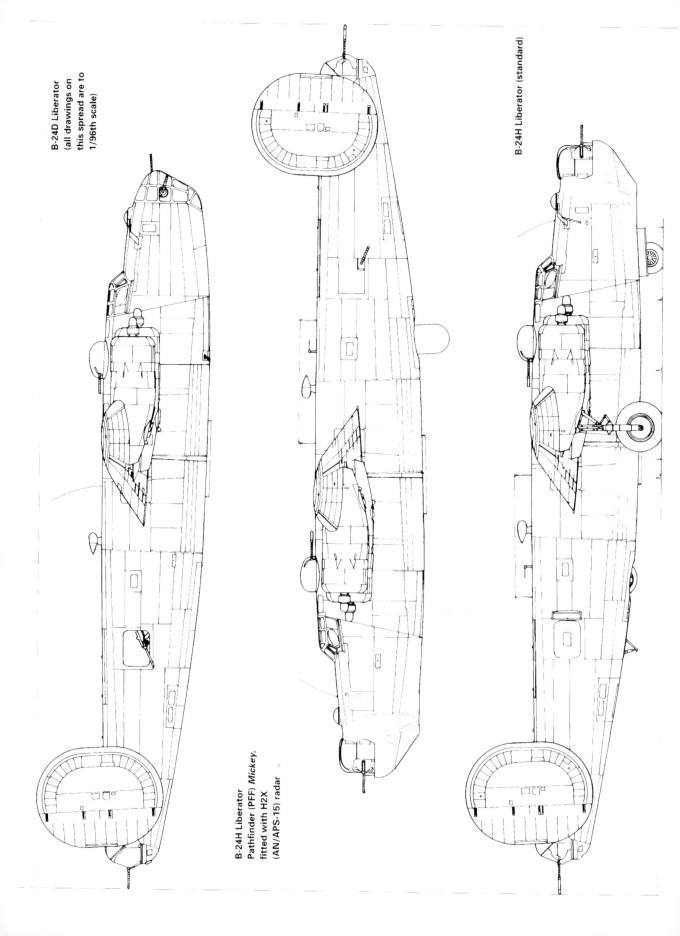

B-24D Liberator
(all drawings on
this spread are to
1/96th scale)

B-24H Liberator
Pathfinder (PFF) *Mickey*,
fitted with H2X
(AN/APS-15) radar

B-24H Liberator (standard)

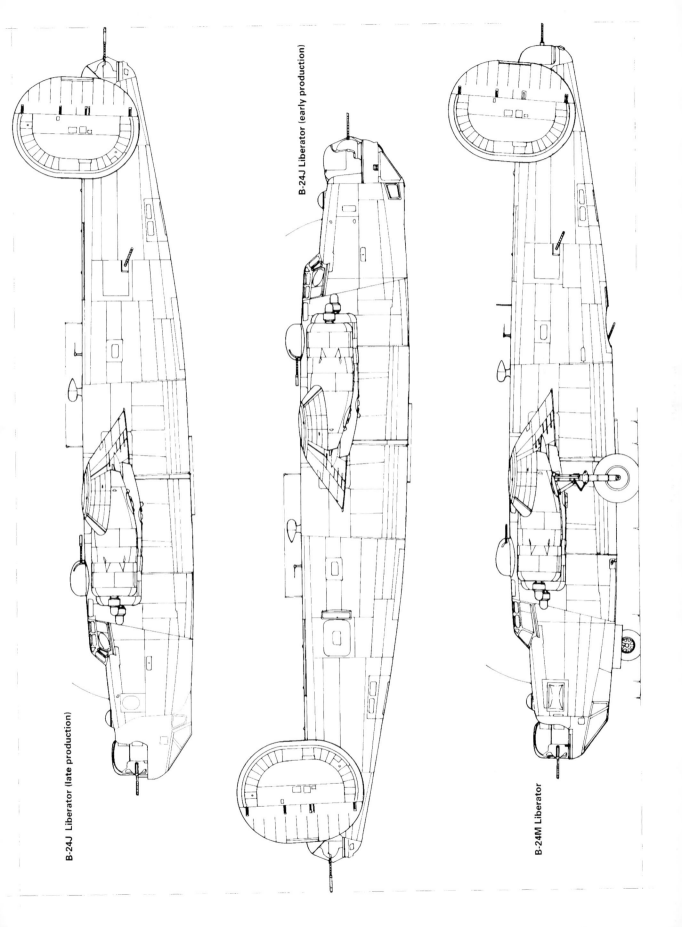

B-24J Liberator (late production)

B-24J Liberator (early production)

B-24M Liberator

COLOUR PLATES

1

B-24D-1-CO 41-23745 *KATY BUG* of the 93rd BG, Alconbury, November 1942

Resplendent in the earliest markings worn by the first Liberators to see combat, this bomber had completed its maiden flight on 24 July 1942 and been delivered to the AAF at San Diego four days later. Apparently part of the original contingent of Liberators from the 93rd BG to take up residence at Alconbury, the bomber had flown into the base in early September 1942. *KATY BUG* was finished in olive-drab and grey, and wore the national insignia authorised for US military aircraft from shortly after Pearl Harbor until June 1943 – namely, a blue roundel enclosing a white star. All of the colours on the aircraft, and especially the national insignia, soon acquired a weathered, worn look in the ETO. The camouflage was worn by extensive use, but the national insignia lost its lustre sooner, after crewmembers oversprayed the white star with grey, fearing that its original appearance was too prominent. It would be another four decades or so before the concept of 'low visibility markings' would come into widespread use. This B-24D carried the early nose armament of three .50-cal. (12.7-mm) hand-held machine-guns. This arrangement was considered to be far from ideal by the crews, especially with regard to the lower gun, which had a limited field of fire and could be depressed, but not elevated. Crews solved the problem on some Liberators by moving the weapon farther up on the nose position, or by adding a second gun.

2

B-24D-25-CO 41-24282 *RUTH-LESS* of the 506th BS/44th BG, Shipdham, summer 1943

Even before this bomber had even left the US, pilot Frank Slough (whose wife was named Ruth) and engineer James Caillier had been awarded a medal for their actions when a crisis arose during a training flight. While practising formation flying, a pilot close by lost control and severed the entire tail assembly of his aircraft when it smashed into the nose of Slough's bomber. The co-pilot panicked and 'abandoned ship', so engineer Caillier took over as co-pilot to help Slough to try to salvage his aeroplane. Despite no forward vision due the other bomber's empennage blocking their view, they managed to locate their base and land successfully. Soon afterward, Slough flew *RUTH-LESS* to England. The Liberator reached the group in March 1943, and completed many tough missions, including a 1 May 1943 raid on Kiel, and (during detached service to Benina Main, in Libya) the famous 1 August assault on oil refineries at Ploesti. On 2 February 1944, *RUTH-LESS* launched from its Shipdham base manned by 1Lt James O Bolin and his crew, who had not yet been assigned a regular aircraft. Their target was to have been a German V1 'buzz bomb' site at Watten, but *RUTH-LESS* experienced engine trouble en route and the crew turned for home, apparently jettisoning their bombs in the English Channel. British police

constable Neville Adams, in Eastbourne, saw the bomber, and noticed how 'the engines were cutting in and out'. A young woman by the name of Audrey Armstrong also heard the engines straining, and later stated that she thought she had seen the face of the pilot as the troubled Liberator broke out of the mist and approached a hill top. Armstrong looked into the pilot's face at the same instant she realised the bomber would not clear the hilltop. The young woman and her companion were nearly hit when *RUTH-LESS* disintegrated in a dry clump, followed by a sharp blast. All on board lost their lives. Had the B-24D had just another 40 ft (12.19 m) of altitude, the crew would have gotten home and survived. Bolin and all ten men on board lost their lives. Today, a small monument to the lost crew of *RUTH-LESS* – erected after nearby resident Kevin Roberts drummed up local support – is painstakingly kept in good order in Eastbourne.

3

B-24D-25-CO 42-24226 *JOISEY BOUNCE* of the 330th BS/93rd BG, Hardwick, summer 1943

This aircraft began its service in the combat zone as *JOISEY BOUNCE* (a musical ditty based on the state of New Jersey) until pilot, Walter Stewart, re-named it in time for the low-level Ploesti mission of 1 August 1943. Built in San Diego, 42-24226 made its initial flight on 20 November 1942, and was delivered to the AAF four days later. The bomber was assigned overseas to the 93rd BG on 17 April 1943, and following its brief existence as *JOISEY BOUNCE*, it became better known by the name assigned by Stewart – *UTAH MAN*. The pilot apparently picked the new appellation for the bomber, then coded AG-L, because another B-24 named *JERSEY BOUNCE* was also assigned to the Ploesti low-level raid. Indeed, it is thought that the latter aircraft actually suffered the first casualty of the historic mission over Romania when its tail gunner was killed by an attacking fighter. *JOISEY BOUNCE/UTAH MAN* was eventually lost on 13 November 1943 on a mission to Bremen with another crew (Stewart had completed his combat tour by then). It failed to return after a mid-air collision with 42-40765 *VALIANT VIRGIN* of the 329th BS/93rd BG, coded RE-T – both aircraft crashed near Husum, Germany. The pilot of 42-24226, 2Lt Loren J Koon, and seven other members of the ten-man crew where killed.

4

B-24D-20-CF 42-63980 *MISSOURI MAULER* of the 567th BS/389th BG, Hethel, summer 1943

This bomber, nicknamed *MISSOURI MAULER* and boasting a 'Q-dash' tail code, was a vintage specimen of the early B-24s produced by the US government's second source for Liberators, namely the Consolidated factory in Fort Worth, Texas. This facility ultimately turned out 3034 of the total of 19,256 of all Liberator models manufactured. This

American record for production of the most aircraft of a single type at the same site held firm until 1999, when the same factory, now owned by Lockheed Martin, produced its 3035th F-16 Fighting Falcon. *MISSOURI MAULER* wore standard olive drab, with light grey undersides, and typical lettering for the 389th BG. Like most early D-models, it carried no ball turret, instead boasting a single, hand-held, stowable gun, mounted in a port on the underside of the rear fuselage. 42-63980 had been accepted into the AAF inventory on 18 August 1943, and arrived overseas on 12 October 1943 – just a few days before the 389th BG resumed operations over western Europe after returning from North Africa, and the famous Ploesti mission. Sometime in early 1944, custody of the Liberator was transferred to the 328th BG at Watton, where it flew with the 36th BS. When the two 'Carpetbagger' squadrons were activated as part of the 801st BG(P) in late March 1944, 42-63980 went with them to Harrington, where it flew many clandestine missions during the peak of the group's activity in the summer of 1944. In November of that same year, the aircraft was selected for an OSS (Office of Strategic Services) trip to 'points east', and on a three-month odyssey travelled to Egypt, New Delhi, Ceylon and Burma (whilst at Myitkina, in the latter country, in January 1945, this much-travelled bomber was spotted wearing 90 mission markers), before returning to Harrington in late January 1945. It then resumed flying 'Carpetbagger' missions out of North Pickenham with the 856th BS/492nd BG. The veteran B-24 was finally flown back to the USA on 9 July 1945.

5
B-24D-30-CO 42-40128 *WAR BABY/BALL OF FIRE THE III* of the 328th BS/93rd BG, Hardwick, autumn 1943

This San Diego-built Liberator carried the nickname *WAR BABY* on the starboard side and *BALL OF FIRE THE III* to port. This profile depicts the aircraft whilst it was piloted by 1Lt Frank Kilcheski. Note its red-bordered 'star and bar' insignia, which was authorised for use for just a few brief weeks in 1943 – most other AAF aircraft had swapped the red for blue by the autumn of 1943. Given its first check flight on 26 December 1942, 42-40128 was delivered to the AAF four days later. It was subsequently flown by Maj Joseph Tate on the most famous Liberator strike of them all – the 1 August 1943 *Tidal Wave* mission against oil refineries in Ploesti. At this time, it was Tate's third aircraft, and was duly named *BALL OF FIRE THE III*. Returning to the UK following its temporary deployment to North Africa, the Liberator sustained damage from attacking Bf 109s during a bombing raid on Hjeller-Oslo, in Norway, on 18 November 1943 and diverted to Sweden. 42-40128 landed at Orebro, but was later flown to Västeras, which served as home for the Swedish Air Force's F 1 Wing. Following almost two years in storage, Swedish officials finally reduced the veteran Liberator to scrap in 1945. The crew of *WAR BABY/BALL OF FIRE THE III* on her final mission (listed here to symbolise all Liberator crews

who fought, since space limitations prevent naming every one) consisted of pilot 1Lt Frank Kilcheski, co-pilot Lt Robert A Hill, navigator Lt Walter H Sills, bombardier Lt Abe H Shonier, engineer Sgt Glenn A Corn, radio operator Sgt Ed Donelly, gunner Sgt Dan Cairns, gunner Sgt James Nichols, gunner Sgt Bertil Carlson and gunner Sgt Bob Bryce. Even after acquiring its *WAR BABY* identity, this Liberator retained Maj Tate's nickname on its left side. The artwork to the left of the *BALL OF FIRE THE III* titling takes the form of a burning billiard ball with a number 8 (for the Eighth Air Force), topped by two bandit caricatures in the form of Japan's Emperor Hirohito and Germany's Adolf Hitler, being symbolically executed. The actual name *BALL OF FIRE THE III* was barely visible.

6
B-24D-20-CO 41-24215 *LUCKY GORDON*, assembly ship for the 445th BG, Tibenham, autumn 1943

Delivered to the AAF on 24 November 1942, this aircraft began its flying career as a standard B-24D, fitted with a 'greenhouse' nose and no turret. In its combat role, the bomber flew as *LUCKY GORDON* with the 93rd BG. Following retirement from 'Ted's Traveling Circus', 41-24215 was transferred to the 445th BG, where it became that group's first assembly ship. In order to fulfil its new role, *LUCKY GORDON* was painted in contrasting black and orange colours. The radio call number ('4124215', which is a rendition of the aircraft's serial number) on the tail is non-standard, and should read '124215'. This aircraft was one of only two such B-24s used by the group, and was replaced sometime in 1944 by a natural-metal finished B-24H. Assembly ships were all combat-weary veterans (initially D-models only) deemed unfit for operational flying. Stripped of armour and armament, they were painted in distinctive colours so as to stand out from other aircraft. Their high visibility would duly allow the crews from a particular group to identify their formation, and slot into place in preparation for the flight into occupied Europe. The importance of this role is described by B-24 navigator Horace Turell;

'The purpose of the assembly ship was for the groups to form up (to begin a mission). The weather in England was the cause. We would typically take off at 30-second intervals if we could see the end of the runway. If not, the take-off interval was increased to 45 seconds. We would usually find ourselves in thick cloud immediately. There were 44 bomb groups assembling in an area half the size of Vermont. Each group flew a racetrack oval from a radio signal, called a "Buncher". When the top of the overcast was reached, usually at over 15,000 ft (4572 m), we would be in bright sunshine. Airplanes would be popping out of the overcast all over. The problem was to find your own group out of the 43 others.

'The assembly ship would be circling over the "Buncher", firing off flares with the groups' colours. Each plane would come up and take its assigned position in the formation. When the formation was complete, or the time deadline reached, the lead would take over and the assembly ship would land.

On several occasions some "eager beavers" flew the unarmed assembly ship with the group to targets close to French coast. This happened on D-Day when Jimmy Stewart (the actor, and commander of the 700th BS/445th BG) took our assembly ship on a raid on the French coast.

'In spite of the bright colours and flares, many B-24s could not locate their group, and consequently attached themselves to another group. The groups then proceeded to another assembly area, where the groups would form up into wings and then depart the English coast, hopefully on time. During assembly, radio silence was strictly observed.'

'The assembly process could, and did, consume two to three hours. Under ideal conditions (I never saw that in England), it could be just one hour. The climb-out was always very hairy. Occasionally, you would see a very bright flash, and you knew it was a mid-air (collision). Frequently during the climb-out, you would get severe propwash, and you knew that it was caused by a near miss. You never saw them. I believe that accidents accounted for 20 per cent of our losses.'

7

B-24H-1-FD 42-7576 *STAR DUST* of the 705th BS/446th BG, Bungay, autumn 1943

This Ford-built B-24H was also known as *BLACK DOG* during its time with the 705th BS/446th BG. Accepted into the AAF inventory on 14 August 1943, the aircraft arrived in the UK on 15 November 1943. It is typical of the first H-model Liberators to reach the Eighth Air Force. 42-7576 is under-stood to have had a prolonged career in the ETO, but records do not confirm whether it survived the war.

8

B-24H-1-FO 42-7549 of the 67th BS/44th BG, Shipdham, November 1943

This Ford-built B-24H had been assigned to the AAF inventory on 13 August 1943, arriving in the UK 17 days later. It evoked numerous memories for 67th BS/44th BG inspector, Will Lundy;

'The bomber was quite familiar to me. I remember when it arrived, and saw it often as it was in dispersal No 37, right next to my aircraft. When our photographic officer, Ursel Harvell, tried to make more money after the war, he printed a small booklet named *Jaws Over Europe*, and featured the nose photo of this plane on the cover. It was nicknamed "The Shark". It was an ex-392nd BG ship, although it had flown no missions with that group. The bomber was received at Shipdham sometime in September 1943 while our combat crews were on detached service to North Africa. It flew its first mission on 9 October 1943. Later, both main landing gears collapsed in one incident, and on 16 June it crash-landed at Woodchurch, near Kingsnorth in Kent, whilst returning from a mission. It was salvaged from 19 to 21 March 1944. "The Shark" flew 33 missions prior to its crash-landing.'

9

B-24D-1-CO 41-23689 *MINERVA*, assembly ship for the 392nd BG, Wendling, January 1944

One of the earliest Liberators to fight in Europe, this San Diego-built aircraft made its initial shakedown flight from the Consolidated factory on 13 July 1942, and was delivered to the AAF five days later. Issued to the 44th BG, *MINERVA* survived the Ploesti raid, and was eventually 'retired' to the 392nd BG in January 1944. Designated an assembly ship (these aircraft were also dubbed 'Judas Goats' by more cynical Eighth Air Force aircrew, as they felt the assembly ships led other B-24s to the slaughter), 41-23689 was painted up in one of the most amazing schemes worn by any Liberator in the ETO. The in-depth repre-sentations of multiple B-24 bombers is similar to a 'disruptive' camouflage scheme that the AAF tested in the United States, but in *MINERVA's* case, it was intended to make the Liberator easier, not harder, to see. The original scheme had been created for use in the Pacific, where it was hoped that it would confuse Japanese observers on the ground into thinking that there were more B-24s in the sky above them than there actually were! However, the idea was abandoned at an early stage, and the 392nd BG subsequently adopted it in an attempt to give pilots a visual indication of how far apart bombers within the formation should be spaced. Unusually for an assembly ship, 41-23689 retained armament in its upper and tail turrets for at least some of the time it served in this role. It was severely damaged in a non-combat mishap sometime in 1944, but was officially salvaged by the 93rd BG on 30 October 1944, and then apparently passed around between several bomb groups. Towards the end of its long career, in April 1945, 41-23689 carried no fewer than 52 men, and their equipment, in an experimental ten-hour flight to determine the feasibility of using bombers to transport ground troops back to the United States at the end of hostilities. Mercifully, the idea of using the B-24 to bring soldiers home after the surrender was quietly set aside.

10

B-24D-5-CO 41-23809 *You cawn't miss it!*, assembly ship for the 448th BG, Seething, February 1944

The last of the three Eighth Air Force B-24 units to go operational in December 1943, the 448th began with standard B-24D models. This B-24D-5-CO was early off the San Diego production line, being delivered to the AAF on 22 August 1942. Like most of the original assembly ships, it had previously served with the 93rd BG (carrying the nickname *Hell's a Droppin II*) in the conventional bombing role. In February 1944 41-23809 was passed to the 448th BG, who stripped it out and painted it in the gaudy colours seen in this profile, transforming it into an assembly ship. The distinctive paint scheme was initially restricted to the fuselage and tail surfaces, but eventually the entire wing area was also adorned with checkerboard squares of yellow and black. In June 1944, the deteriorating mechanical condition of the veteran bomber saw it replaced by B-24D 42-63981 *The Striped Ape*. The role of the assembly ship has been little understood in the language of the Liberator. To quote another veteran, pilot John Jakab remembers it this way;

'Assembling a group formation was, on occasion, a stressful and hazardous endeavour. When temperature and dew point were equal, or nearly equal, the ships departing the base and climbing to formation altitude would start producing vapour trails from about 1500 ft (457 m) to 2000 ft (610 m). Considering that there were many groups taking off at about the same time, the vapour trails could form a solid overcast over East Anglia that was 15,000 ft (4572 m) to 20,000 ft (6096 m) thick. The planes would usually break out above the overcast at about 16,000 ft (4876 m) to 19,000 ft (5791 m).

'During the climb, the planes flew a specified racetrack pattern on the group's assigned "buncher", or radio facility, until they reached their assigned altitude. If visual flight rules could be maintained, the group would assume their formation positions on the assembly aircraft. If visual flight rules could not be maintained at the assigned altitude, the aircraft would proceed to the next assigned radio beacon, climbing to a higher assigned altitude, or until reaching visual conditions. After the group was in formation, the mission leader would take the lead position, and the assembly aircraft would depart and return to the base.

'Of course, when weather was not a factor, assembly in formation was relatively easy. In every case radio silence was maintained. If someone made a radio transmission for whatever reason, no one would reply. Some communication was accomplished by using Very pistol flares. Occasionally, we had mid-air collisions and aborting aircraft for mechanical problems, but we seldom knew of them unless they were in our own unit.

'I do recall an incident that occurred when my crew was not scheduled to fly. I went to the control tower to watch the planes take-off. One of the B-24s evidently had a loose fuel cap on the right wing behind No 3 engine, and fuel was being siphoned out behind the plane. Its pilot broke radio silence by declaring an emergency and requesting landing instructions. However, the tower did not respond. After circling the field a couple of times without receiving any response, someone in the plane decided to fire a red-red flare to indicate an emergency. Unfortunately, the Very pistol port was on the right side of the fuselage and the flare went up, then descended into the stream of siphoned fuel. The fuel ignited, and when the flame reached the wing, the plane exploded. There were no survivors. It was unforgettable.'

Not that everyone noticed the bombers forming up. Navigator Horace Turell remembers;

'During climb out and assembly I had my head inside the *Gee* box so I could tell the crew if we were over water in the event of bailout. I was also trying my damnedest to get a wind reading to check the meteorological forecast. So one eye was on the *Gee* screen and another eye was watching the compass and airspeed. The "third eye" was whipping the E6B (navigator's slide rule device) around, and the "fourth eye" was watching my "third hand" make log

entries! The only time I ever had for sightseeing was on the bomb run, and during take-offs and landings. So the assembly ships were colourful, but I hardly ever paid any attention to one.'

11

B-24J-155-CO 44-40275 *"Shack Time"* of the 753rd BS/458th BG, Horsham St Faith, spring 1944

This San Diego-built Consolidated B-24J is an example of the ultimate version of the Liberator which, after combat experience and developmental work, was able to range over Europe enjoying considerable protection from its own fire power – so much so that one Luftwaffe fighter pilot compared attacking a late-model B-24 to 'making love to a porcupine'. 44-40275 made its first flight on 14 March 1944 and was delivered to the AAF three days later. Its final disposition is not recorded.

12

B-24H-15-CO 42-52559 *Miss Fortune* of the 790th BS/467th BG, Rackheath, spring 1944

Piloted for much of its time in the frontline by 1Lt Richard E Evans, this B-24 was accepted into the AAF inventory on 22 December 1943 and arrived in the UK on 13 March 1944. Its combat career was a truncated one, lasting a little more than four months during a time of heavy fighting over the continent which also witnessed the first missions to Berlin. On 12 July 1944, *Miss Fortune* sustained battle damage, forcing Evans to perform an emergency landing at Dübendorf, in Switzerland, where both the bomber and crew were interned.

13

B-24H-20-CF 42-95011 of the 856th BS/492nd BG, North Pickenham, May 1944

A Fort Worth-built Liberator, this aircraft flew in the colours of the 856th BS on a critical mission on 29 May 1944, although there is dispute as to whether it was regularly assigned to the squadron. That day, the target was Politz, and the Liberator was hit by anti-aircraft fire, which wounded the engineer, making him unable to transfer fuel. Others in the crew did not normally know how to perform this complex function, but in this instance pilot, 2Lt Gaulke, had taken an interest in the mechanical functions of his Liberator, and was able to transfer enough fuel to divert to Rinkaby military airfield near Khristanstad, in Sweden, where nose gunner, Sgt Warren G Branch Jr, and others, assisted the pilot in making a landing. To help get the aircraft down at what proved to be a frighteningly short airstrip, Branch and ball turret gunner Sgt Francis Baker attached their parachutes to the waist gun mounts and released them on touchdown. Sgt Baker's 'chute pulled his gun out of the aircraft, along with his low-quarter shoes, which had been tied to the weapon! The Liberator halted with less than 100 ft (30 m) to spare at runway's end. The crew was interned. However, Sweden was now leaning heavily toward the Allied cause (much as, earlier, it had leaned toward the German cause when the latter were winning), so both this Liberator and its crew were repatriated early on 24 October 1944. Branch, typical of those who survived internment, went on to become a gunnery instructor in B-29 Superfortresses. 42-95011 was flown back to the USA from England on 11 June 1945.

14

B-24J-5-FO 42-50829 of the 330th BS/93rd BG, Hardwick, summer 1944

Another product of Ford's relentless Willow Run factory, this B-24J was typical of the early J-models that began to reach the Eighth Air Force in 1944. Never given a name, the bomber was accepted into the inventory on 25 May 1944, and reached 'Ted's Traveling Circus' in England on 22 July. Like so many Liberators during those intense months of battle, it was not around for long. On 18 September 1944, while being piloted by Maj Howard K Segars on a supply drop to Allied airborne troops in the Nether-lands, this bomber ditched in the North Sea 37 miles (60 km) from Orfordness, Suffolk.

15

B-24H-25-DT 42-51128 *UMBRIAGO* of the 579th BS/392nd BG, Wendling, summer 1944

Assembled at the Douglas plant in Tulsa, Oklahoma, this Liberator was accepted into the AAF inventory on 19 February 1944, and arrived overseas on 18 April. 42-51128 was a pathfinder aircraft, fitted with a retractable H2X radome. It was battle damaged on 16 November 1944 on a mission to Eschweiler, and was salvaged on the continent. *UMBRIAGO*, which was one of no fewer than thirteen Liberators to bear this popular name, appears to have survived the war.

16

B-24H-15-CF 41-29487 *BLASTED EVENT!* of the 700th BS/445th BG, Tibenham, summer 1944

This Fort Worth-built Liberator seems to have been a good luck charm for those tasked to take it into battle, for it appears that *BLASTED EVENT!* made the journey back and forth over the Third Reich more frequently than most other bombers in the group. And on each occasion it brought its crew home safely. 41-29487 made its first flight on 5 January 1944, and was delivered to the AAF three days later. Upon the bomber's arrival in England, it was issued to the 487th BG, within the 3rd Air Division (which ultimately divested itself of Liberators), before transferring to the 2nd Air Division's 445th BG at Tibenham. 41-29487 was salvaged as 'war weary' on 29 May 1945 by the 3rd Air Base Depot.

17

B-24H-20-FO 42-94921 *"TAHELENBAK"* of the 701st BS/445th BG, Tibenham, summer 1944

This Ford-built B-24H was given its name as a word play on the name of a woman, coupled with what many Liberator crews felt they were doing over the Third Reich – literally travelling to Hell and back. The bomber was accepted into the AAF inventory on 3 March 1944, and reached England on 26 April. With little fanfare, 42-94921 completed its missions, survived the war, and returned to the USA.

18

B-24H-15-FO 42-52594 *NAUGHTY NAN* of the 705th BS/446th BG, Bungay, summer 1944

This Ford-built H-model was accepted into the Army Air Force's inventory on 28 December 1943, and is listed as having been assigned overseas on 11 March 1944. Christened *NAUGHTY NAN* (and possibly given the name *NAUGHTY NAN II* at a later date), the bomber completed 55 combat missions before being written off in a crash-landing at Bungay on 13 November 1944. Although AAF records also show that the aircraft was 'salvaged' on 20 December 1944, this does not mean that it was restored to flying status. *NAUGHTY NAN* was a popular nickname within the Eighth Air Force, with a second so-named Liberator (B-24J-5-FO 42-51543) being operated concurrently alongside 42-52594 within the 705th BS! The latter bomber had been accepted into the inventory on 29 June 1944 and assigned overseas on 26 August 1944. It survived the war, and is listed as having ended its career at the outdoor storage facility in Kingman.

19

B-24H-15-FO 42-94759 *The Sharon D.* of the 489th BG, Halesworth, summer 1944

This Ford-built B-24H was assigned to Lt Col Leon Vance, deputy commander of the 489th BG. It was Vance who had brought the aircraft from the US to Halesworth. The bomber was named after its pilot's infant daughter Sharon, who had been born in 1942. Lt Col Vance was flying a different aircraft on the 5 June 1944 mission against a German coastal defence complex near Wimereaux, France – a mission in which the latter aircraft was lost, and for which Vance was awarded the Medal of Honor. He was the only B-24 crew member in the Eighth Air Force accorded this distinction whilst flying a mission from the UK. Vance was heading home to recover from combat wounds when he went down on a C-54 Skymaster carrying wounded and crippled veterans over the North Atlantic on 26 July 1944. In October 1946, at the age of four, Sharon Vance travelled via US Army Air Forces transport to Enid, Oklahoma (now home of Vance Air Force Base), for a ceremony in which Maj Gen James P Hodges gave her the Medal of Honor awarded to her father. Today, daughter Sharon Kiernan of San Diego, California, is an Air Force wife, and she helps to keep alive the memory of her father, and of the bomber named after her. *The Sharon D.* retained its nickname throughout the war, and was eventually transferred to the 445th BG. It survived the conflict, and was eventually broken up for scrap.

20

B-24J-145-CO 44-40073 *ARK ANGEL* of the 853rd BS/491st BG, Metfield, summer 1944

This Liberator was delivered from San Diego on 1 March 1944, and after arriving in the UK on 16 May 1944, it was assigned as original equipment to the 491st BG. The bomber's pilot was Linus J Box, who hailed from Fort Worth, Texas. Something of an artist, he actually painted the *ARK ANGEL* onto 44-40073 – the crew also had the same painting on their A2 leather jackets, and one of these, which belonged to bombardier, Roy Hall, is presently on display at the Lone Star Flight Museum in Galveston, Texas. The Liberator flew its first mission on 2 June 1944, and its brief role in the war ended when it was one of 15 B-24s from the 491st BG shot down by German fighters on 26 November on a raid to Misburg, Germany. On this mission ARK ANGEL was flown by 1Lt David N Bennett Jr and crew, all of whom were killed in action. Their targets on this day were rail viaducts, marshalling yards and oil installations in western Germany, and the bombers were opposed by no fewer than 500 enemy fighters. The story behind this aircraft may not be over yet, however, for a German farmer has recently located the site where ARK ANGEL crashed on his grandfather's property near the town of Oeire – he has done some excavating and uncovered artefacts. As a symbolic gesture toward all who were killed serving with B-24 Liberator units of the Eighth Air Force, the lost crew of ARK ANGEL consisted of: pilot, 1Lt David N Bennett Jr, of Norwood North Carolina; co-pilot, 2Lt Jesse F Blount, of Gainesville Texas; navigator, 2Lt George H Engel, of Pittsburg Pennsylvania; nose turret gunner, S/Sgt Irving B Starr, of Brooklyn, New York; top turret gunner, T/Sgt Norman G Warford, of Frankfort, New York; radio operator, T/Sgt Pete Patrick Jr, of East Point, New York; left waist gunner, S/Sgt Raymond O McKee, of Baton Rouge, Louisiana; right waist gunner, S/Sgt Charles E Hixon, of Cleveland, Tennessee; and tail gunner, S/Sgt Henry P Stovall, of Beckley, West Virginia. All honour to their names.

21
B-24H-15-FO 42-52768 *LEO* of the 860th BS/493rd BG, Debach, summer 1944

LEO, christened in honour of the cartoon world's famous lion of the same name, was a Ford-built B-24H-15-FO, and it came out of the factory in standard olive-drab with light grey undersides. This bomber was originally assigned to the 834th BS (known as the 'Zodiac' squadron) within the 486th BG at Sudbury. For a long time after acquiring its colourful nose art, nickname and K code letter upon joining the 860th BS/493rd BG, the bomber also retained a hint of its painted-out '2S' identification marking, which was barely capable of being discerned on the rear fuselage. Aside from adding the single-letter tail code, the 860th BS also painted the B-24's propeller hubs in its trademark yellow. The 493rd BG was part of the 93rd Combat Bomb Wing, and was one of the Liberator units which was pressured into transferring onto the B-17 Flying Fortress in September 1944. Known as 'Helton's Hellcats' after its long-serving Group CO, Col Elbert Helton, the 493rd BG operated from Debach (Station 152), in Suffolk, from April 1944 through to August 1945. The group clearly enjoyed the talents of a superb (but sadly anonymous) artist, since a number of its B-24s wore individual caricatures of the same high quality as *LEO*.

22
B-24J-145-CO 44-40101 *TUBARAO* of the 854th BS/491st BG, North Pickenham, September 1944

Nicknamed *TUBARAO*, which is Portuguese for shark, this Liberator made its first flight on 23 February 1944 and was delivered to the AAF five days later. Assigned to the 854th BS/491st BG, with 2Lt Wilson W Waggoner as its pilot, the bomber initially wore the code 6X-D until August 1944, when it became 6X-A. After being damaged in September 1944, and after being repaired, was assigned to the 855th BS/491st BG as V2-O+. After completing just 20 missions in its final six months in the frontline, *TUBARAO* was declared 'war-weary' in January 1945 and converted into the 491st's third assembly ship – it replaced B-24J-150-CO 44-40165 *RAGE IN HEAVEN*, which had crashed and been destroyed whilst attempting to take off in a snow storm from North Pickenham on 5 January 1945.

23
B-24H-25-FO 42-95049 *Fearless Fosdick/writ by hand* of the 67th BS/44th BG, Shipdham, autumn 1944

This Willow Run-built aircraft was never painted, appearing in natural metal from the time it rolled out of the factory until 1 March 1945, when it was lost on a mission after running out of fuel. *Fearless Fosdick* was the name of a character in the Al Capp cartoon strip *L'il Abner*, and was, in turn, a spoof of another cartoon strip hero in the shape of Chester Goold's famous *Dick Tracy*. 42-95049 was accepted into the AAF inventory on 2 March 1944, and arrived in England on 23 April 1944. It spent the following 11 months assigned to the venerable 'Flying Eightballs' at Shipdham, before being abandoned on the continent while returning from a mission to Ingolstadt.

24
B-24J-5-DT 42-51376 of the 329th BS/93rd BG, Hardwick, autumn 1944

Built by Douglas in Tulsa, this B-24J fought a long and hard war without ever attracting much attention from those who take notes. Delivered in 1944, and arriving at Hardwick that same year, 42-51376 seems to have avoided any significant claims to fame, except the only one that matters – when it was over and done, this Liberator survived the war and returned to the USA.

25
B-24J-65-CF 44-10599 *WiNDY WiNNiE* of the 712th BS/448th BG, Seething, autumn 1944

The career of this bomber began with a shakedown flight on 23 June 1944, followed by acceptance by the AAF three days later. During the bomb group's tour in England, it had two aircraft named *WiNDY WiNNiE*, the first being B-24J-1-FO 42-50676, which flew with the 712th BS. Like other squadrons in the 448th BG, this unit marked its aircraft with a geometric shape – in this instance a triangle. The 448th did not conform to normal Eighth Air Force practice, for it began using geometric shapes to indicate squadrons as soon as it arrived in-theatre. The group marking was the 'circle I'. Sometime shortly after the 448th started its tour, the Eighth adapted the two-digit squadron call letters – the 712th's call letters were CT, although the 448th continued to use the geometric shapes as well as the call letters. In May 1944 the group switched to the new group tail marking of yellow tail fins with a black diagonal band, and the 448th placed the squadron geometric code and aircraft call letter in the centre of the band. The group retained the two-digit squadron codes on the aft fuselage until sometime in 1945, and then removed them from most of their aircraft. The 448th was probably one of the only groups in the Eighth to delete the two-digit call letters. 44-10599 was lost during a mission to Dortmund on 28 January 1945.

26

B-24H-20-FO 42-94805 *FOIL PROOF* of the 735th BS/453rd BG, Old Buckenham, autumn 1944
This Ford-built B-24H-20-FO completed no fewer than 111 combat missions and survived the war. It was accepted into the AAF's inventory on 24 February 1944, assigned overseas on 12 April 1944 and 'gained' by the Eighth Air Force on 24 April. There is conflicting information on the early role of this Liberator, which appears to have originally served with the 93rd BG, before transferring to the 453rd BG on a date that, unfortunately, is recorded in official records as '0-0-44'! Upon its arrival at Old Buckenham in late April, *FOIL PROOF* was initially assigned to the 735th BS as a replacement aircraft. The squadron code on the fuselage was H6, and its call letter shown on the vertical stabiliser was U, followed by a plus sign. The plus was soon changed to a bar which, from mid-July 1944, was placed under the letter. The aircraft remained with the 735th BS until the end of March 1945 when, in common with all other non-PFF aircraft in the unit, it was transferred to one of the other three squadrons – in this instance the 733rd BS. *FOIL PROOF* probably retained call letter U following the transfer, although the bar under the letter would have been replaced by a plus sign, positioned to the right of the U. This bomber was noted at one point in olive drab, with markings denoting that it had completed 54 of its eventual 111 missions. It was eventually flown back to Altus, Oklahoma, on 25 September 1945.

27

B-24J-150-CO 44-40201 *Silver Chief* of the 753rd BS/458th BG, Horsham St Faith, autumn 1944
Yet another San Diego-built B-24J, 44-40201 made its first flight on 4 March 1944 and was delivered to the AAF five days later. It arrived in the UK on 26 April 1944, where it became one of the original aircraft assigned to the 492nd BG at North Pickenham (which disbanded on 12 August 1944 to form the genesis of the special operations, or 'Carpetbagger', group, the 801st BG). *Silver Chief* completed only three missions with its original combat group before being reassigned to the 458th BG, where it initially flew as an Azon bomb deliverer (with three distinctive aerial masts beneath the rear fuselage) until such operations were terminated. The bomber continued to serve with the 458th BG until it was salvaged as battle damaged on the continent on 26 January 1945.

28

B-24J-145-CO 44-40117 *HARE POWER* of the 852nd BS/491st BG, North Pickenham, autumn 1944
Built at Consolidated's San Diego factory, 44-40117 made its maiden flight on 25 February 1944 and was delivered to the AAF four days later. An original 491st aircraft that was supplied to the group just prior to its move to the UK, *HARE POWER* was flown by 1Lt Robert G Bennett. It was destroyed on the 26 November 1944 mission to Misburg, the 491st losing no fewer than 16 B-24s to Luftwaffe fighters during the raid. The pilot on its last mission was 1Lt Floyd I Weitz, and although he and two others successfully bailed out and were captured, the remaining six crewmen were killed. The last report the 491st had on the aircraft was that it was seen going down with the bomb bay on fire. The crew bailed out, but apparently nobody in the 491st saw the 'chutes.

29

B-24J-155-CO 44-40317 *Ruthless Ruthie* of the 854th BS/491st BG, North Pickenham, autumn 1944
Like numerous other B-24s, this San Diego-built bomber from the 854th BS/491st BG 'The Ringmasters' shared its nickname with several other Liberators. 44-40317 first flew on 20 March 1944, and was turned over to the AAF 48 hours later. It reached England on 19 May, and appears to have been assigned to another bomb group, before showing up on 'The Ringmasters'' roster in September 1944. After nearly a year of success, *Ruthless Ruthie* blew a left tyre while taking off for a mission to the Landshuit marshalling yards on 16 April 1945 (one of the last big Liberator efforts of the war) and careened off the runway about 400 ft (120 m) later. It ran across rough ground for another 500 ft (155 m), before its right gear collapsed and the aircraft came to an awkward halt. Eighth Air Force records list the bomber as being salvaged that same date.

30

B-24M-5-FO 44-50527 *HAZEE* of the 732nd BS/453rd BG, Old Buckenham, spring 1945
This aircraft is typical of the later model Liberators that swarmed over Europe in the final days of the war. 44-50527 was accepted into the AAF inventory on 9 January 1945, and promptly arrived overseas on 7 February. The bomber served initially with the 577th BS/392nd BG at Wendling, before being passed on to the 453rd BG. It survived the war and returned to the USA soon after VE-Day.

INDEX

References to illustrations are shown in **bold**.
Plates are shown with page and caption locators
in brackets.